Explainable
Natural Language Processing

Synthesis Lectures on Human Language Technologies

Editor
Graeme Hirst, *University of Toronto*

Synthesis Lectures on Human Language Technologies is edited by Graeme Hirst of the University of Toronto. The series consists of 50- to 150-page monographs on topics relating to natural language processing, computational linguistics, information retrieval, and spoken language understanding. Emphasis is on important new techniques, on new applications, and on topics that combine two or more HLT subfields.

Explainable Natural Language Processing
Anders Søgaard
2021

Finite-State Text Processing
Kyle Gorman and Richard Sproat
2021

Semantic Relations Between Nominals, Second Edition
Vivi Nastase, Stan Szpakowicz, Preslav Nakov, and Diarmuid Ó Séagdha
2021

Embeddings in Natural Language Processing: Theory and Advances in Vector Representations of Meaning
Mohammad Taher Pilehvar and Jose Camacho-Collados
2020

Conversational AI: Dialogue Systems, Conversational Agents, and Chatbots
Michael McTear
2020

Natural Language Processing for Social Media, Third Edition
Anna Atefeh Farzindar and Diana Inkpen
2020

Statistical Significance Testing for Natural Language Processing
Rotem Dror, Lotem Peled, Segev Shlomov, and Roi Reichart
2020

Linked Lexical Knowledge Bases: Foundations and Applications
Iryna Gurevych, Judith Eckle-Kohler, and Michael Matuschek
2016

Bayesian Analysis in Natural Language Processing
Shay Cohen
2016

Metaphor: A Computational Perspective
Tony Veale, Ekaterina Shutova, and Beata Beigman Klebanov
2016

Grammatical Inference for Computational Linguistics
Jeffrey Heinz, Colin de la Higuera, and Menno van Zaanen
2015

Automatic Detection of Verbal Deception
Eileen Fitzpatrick, Joan Bachenko, and Tommaso Fornaciari
2015

Natural Language Processing for Social Media
Atefeh Farzindar and Diana Inkpen
2015

Semantic Similarity from Natural Language and Ontology Analysis
Sébastien Harispe, Sylvie Ranwez, Stefan Janaqi, and Jacky Montmain
2015

Learning to Rank for Information Retrieval and Natural Language Processing, Second Edition
Hang Li
2014

Ontology-Based Interpretation of Natural Language
Philipp Cimiano, Christina Unger, and John McCrae
2014

Automated Grammatical Error Detection for Language Learners, Second Edition
Claudia Leacock, Martin Chodorow, Michael Gamon, and Joel Tetreault
2014

Web Corpus Construction
Roland Schäfer and Felix Bildhauer
2013

Recognizing Textual Entailment: Models and Applications
Ido Dagan, Dan Roth, Mark Sammons, and Fabio Massimo Zanzotto
2013

Explainable Natural Language Processing

Anders Søgaard

ISBN: 978-3-031-01052-1   paperback
ISBN: 978-3-031-02180-0   ebook
ISBN: 978-3-031-00191-8   hardcover

DOI 10.1007/978-3-031-02180-0

A Publication in theSpringer series
SYNTHESIS LECTURES ON HUMAN LANGUAGE TECHNOLOGIES

Lecture #51
Series Editor: Graeme Hirst, *University of Toronto*
Series ISSN
Print 1947-4040   Electronic 1947-4059

Explainable
Natural Language Processing

Anders Søgaard
University of Copenhagen

SYNTHESIS LECTURES ON HUMAN LANGUAGE TECHNOLOGIES #51

ABSTRACT

This book presents a taxonomy framework and survey of methods relevant to explaining the decisions and analyzing the inner workings of Natural Language Processing (NLP) models. The book is intended to provide a snapshot of Explainable NLP, though the field continues to rapidly grow. The book is intended to be both readable by first-year M.Sc. students and interesting to an expert audience. The book opens by motivating a focus on providing a consistent taxonomy, pointing out inconsistencies and redundancies in previous taxonomies. It goes on to present (i) a taxonomy or framework for thinking about how approaches to explainable NLP relate to one another; (ii) brief surveys of each of the classes in the taxonomy, with a focus on methods that are relevant for NLP; and (iii) a discussion of the inherent limitations of some classes of methods, as well as how to best evaluate them. Finally, the book closes by providing a list of resources for further research on explainability.

KEYWORDS

natural language processing, interpretability, explainability, taxonomies, resources

Contents

Acknowledgments

The book's shortcomings are entirely my fault. I would nevertheless like to thank my editors and reviewers, as well as several of my colleagues for engaging in discussions that helped shape this book: Mostafa Abdou, Jasmijn Bastings, Katja Filippova, Ana Valeria Gonzalez, Daniel Herschcovich, Karthikeyan K, Anna Rogers, and Anna Rumshinsky. The framework presented here is probably applicable outside of NLP, but I willfully ignore all other applications of interpretability and explainable machine learning throughout the book.

Anders Søgaard
September 2021

CHAPTER 1

Introduction

Explainable Natural Language Processing (NLP)[1] is a new subfield of NLP, only really taking off within the last four or five years.[2] Whenever a new subfield of a scientific discipline emerges, it almost by definition attracts a mixed crowd of researchers from related, but different subfields. These researchers of course do not yet form a consolidated network and also typically bring slightly different traditions, languages, and protocols from their respective subfields. This, undoubtedly, leads to a lot of redundancy: researchers presenting what is essentially the same, in radically different ways; researchers reinventing what they did not know already existed; and researchers proposing new models that only in the absence of established evaluation protocols, seem superior to existing ones.

This book first and foremost presents a taxonomy of approaches to explainable (neural) NLP. I present this taxonomy with the noble, yet perhaps not so humble, goal of accelerating progress in this emerging subfield. I want to make it easier for researchers to relate existing approaches and to monitor the development of new ones, and to provide a common language for talking about explanations in the context of contemporary NLP research. I also briefly survey representative samples of existing work on explainable NLP, as well as discuss principled ways of evaluating such work. I will not be interested in the models that are being interpreted, and what we have learned about them (no Bertology here!), only in different *methods* for deriving explanations and how they are related.

Why are taxonomies important? In Chapter 12, I will derive some general results about interpretability methods from the taxonomy presented here and hopefully thereby convince you that the taxonomy is practically useful. In biology, taxonomies are a form of book-keeping device that primarily is intended to single out important dimensions along which living creatures differ, and possibly provide a useful way of thinking about fauna as a whole.[3] In engineering, I believe taxonomies play additional roles: they are vehicles for thinking about what is possible, and what is not, identifying options that no one yet considered, as well as

---

[1] A brief word on terminology is appropriate: I will use the words explainable and interpretable somewhat interchangeably. If anything, I will follow Clinciu and Hastie (2019) in defining "interpretability as intersecting with explainability as some models may be interpretable without needing explanations," but I generally do not think it is practically important to worry too much about the exact difference, if any, between these terms.

[2] While some of the methods discussed here are somewhat older than that, the oldest being from 1989 (Church and Hanks, 1989), explainable NLP only became an independent track at the Association for Computational Linguistics's main conference in 2020, and was not represented by independent workshops until 2018 (Alishahi et al., 2019).

[3] This is not entirely fair to biology. Biological taxonomies provide a basis for conservation and development, for example, and can possibly be used to generate interesting scientific questions about missing species; see Bacher (2012), for example.

establishing formal relations between existing methods. This is exactly the motivation behind this book: I want to make it easier to see what open problems are left for explainable NLP, what methods are useful to compare (and how), what methods may be mathematically related, and what properties apply to what methods.

The taxonomy is presented in Chapter 2 (§2.2–2.5). It is two-dimensional:

(a) Its first dimension relates to the data requirements of the interpretability method itself, namely whether it requires a representative sample of data points or not. As we will see, this correlates with a number of other differences, including whether the interpretability method *modifies* the model it aims to explain, typically adding extra parameters, and whether the method is motivated by an interest in general model characterization or an interest in worst-case behavior on particularly problematic instances. We call this dimension **local-global**, in line with most previous work, referring to whether you are interested in characterizing the model's decision boundary locally or globally: local methods are typically interested in worst-case behavior or behavior on specific samples; global methods typically train new parameters on larger samples to evaluate the learned representations globally.

(b) The second dimension is where our taxonomy differs from previous work: while most previous taxonomies distinguish between intrinsic and post-hoc methods (see below), we distinguish between those that rely on **forward** passes over the parameters, and those that rely on **backward** passes.

Some examples are easy to place in this taxonomy: using vanilla gradients to highlight which parts of an input are most responsible for a prediction (Denil et al., 2014) clearly falls into the class of *local* approaches that rely on *backward* passes. In contrast, attention head pruning (Voita et al., 2019), for example, falls into the class of *global* approaches that focus on *forward* passes. While attention head pruning does not involve extra parameters, it requires further training based on a sample of representative data. Other approaches are slightly harder to classify, perhaps.[4] Other papers combine methods from two or more classes in the taxonomy presented here,

---

[4]Analogies, for example, i.e., quadruples of concepts that relate in a pairwise, analogous fashion, e.g., *Berlin is to Germany as Copenhagen is to Denmark*, are used to probe and evaluate word embeddings and language models. In a language model, words and phrases are represented by vectors, and if the relationship between the two pairs of vectors was completely analogous, the following would hold: **berlin** − **germany** = **copenhagen** − **denmark**. In practice, we say a language model exhibits analogous encoding if the nearest neighbor of **berlin** − **germany** + **copenhagen** (ignoring any of the three input words) is **denmark**. Analogies have been used to evaluate the global consistency of language models (Garneau et al., 2021) and the extent to which they encode for semantic relations between concepts (Mikolov et al., 2013a). This obviously concerns the *continuous outputs* of language models, i.e., word vectors rather than discrete output (masked or next words). However, at first it may seem that analogies are *global* evaluation methods, because researchers have often used relatively large analogy datasets (Drozd et al., 2016) when evaluating models. We, however, classify analogies as *local* methods, and the reason is simple, yet important for understanding the taxonomy presented here: while large collections of analogies can be used to collect aggregate statistics that say something about models beyond their local decision boundaries, we can also use a single analogy such as the above to infer something about whether these four words were encoded analogously. You will see this throughout this book: local methods can be used to collect aggregate statistics from samples of data, but unlike global methods, they do *not require* samples of data.

either because they compare different methods (Rei and Søgaard, 2018) or because their methods are composed of different steps, e.g., the two-stage methods in Ribeiro et al. (2018), Sushil et al. (2018), MAME (Ramamurthy et al., 2020), etc. In this book, we will generally not discuss two-stage methods. See Chapter 12 (§12.2) for a discussion of what the book omits.

1.1   TWO COMMON DISTINCTIONS

Explainable NLP has only been an active research field for a few years, and only recently have there been attempts to consolidate and systematically compare such research. The simplest taxonomies presented for interpretability methods are one-dimensional, i.e., simple groupings (Atanasova et al., 2020a; Kotonya and Toni, 2020). Other methods introduce several discrete dimensions and use these to cross-classify existing methods. The taxonomies with most dimensions introduce four (4) dimensions (Carvalho et al., 2019; Guidotti et al., 2018; Molnar, 2019). The 10 taxonomies discussed in this section are at most a couple of years old. Two are from 2019 (Carvalho et al., 2019; Molnar, 2019), the rest from 2020 or 2021. I discuss them in roughly chronological order below. First, however, I will discuss two common distinctions that are largely agreed upon: *local-global*, i.e., the distinction between local and global interpretability methods, which is shared among *all* of the eight multi-dimensional taxonomies in Figure 1.1; and *intrinsic-post-hoc*, i.e., the distinction between between intrinsic and post-hoc interpretability methods, which is shared among 7/8 of the multi-dimensional taxonomies. I will argue that one of these distinctions, local-global, is useful, while the other is problematic in several respects.

1.1.1   LOCAL AND GLOBAL EXPLANATIONS

The distinction between local and global interpretability methods is shared across all the taxonomies discussed in this chapter, and will also be one of the two dimensions in the taxonomy I propose below. The distinction is defined slightly differently by different authors,[5] or not defined at all, e.g., Guidotti et al. (2018), but here I present the definition that the taxonomy proposed below relies on:

Definition 1.1   Local-Global.   An interpretability method is said to be *global* if and only if its explanations rely on access to an (i.i.d.) *sample* of representative instances; otherwise, if the method can provide explanations for individual instances in the absence of such samples, it is said to be *local*.

---

[5]Danilevsky et al. (2020), for example, says that *a local explanation provides information or justification for the model's prediction on a specific input, [while] a global explanation provides similar justification by revealing how the model's predictive process works, independently of any particular input.* As should be clear from the discussion below, this is not equivalent to our definition, which uses the reliance of global methods on samples, rather than the reliance of local methods on specific instances, as the distinguishing criterion. One argument against the definition in Danilevsky et al. (2020) is that it is not entirely clear in what sense global methods such as concept activation vectors (Kim et al., 2018), for example, are *independent of any particular input.* The function that provides us with explanations is global, but of course its output depends on the input.

	Guidotti et al. (2018)	Adadi and Berrada (2018)	Carvalho et al. (2019)	Molnar (2019)	Zhang et al. (2020)	Danilevsky et al. (2020)	Das and Rad (2020)
GradCAM	L				L-H		L-H
DeepLift	H				L-H		L-H
LRP		L/G-H			S-H	L-I/H	L/G-H
LIME	L	L-H	L-H	L	L-H	L-H	L/G-H
TCAV				G-I	G-H		G-H
IF			L/G	L-H			

Explanation: local (L), global (G), intrinsic (I), and post-hoc (H).

(a)

	Forward	Backward
Local	Attention, Attention roll-out, Attention flow, Time step dynamics, Local uptraining, Influence functions	Gradients, Layer-wise relevance propagation, Deep Taylor decomposition, Integrated gradients, DeepLift
Global	Weight pruning, Correlation of representations, Clustering, Probing classifiers, Uptraining	Dynamic sparse training, Binary networks, Sparse coding, Concept activation, Gradient-based weight pruning

(b)

Figure 1.1: (a) 4/6 methods (bottom half) are classified incoherently across taxonomies. *Explanation:* local (L), global (G), intrinsic (I), and post-hoc (H). (b) our novel taxonomy.

Note that the definition does not refer to how the methods characterize the models, e.g., whether they describe individual inferences, or derive aggregate statistics that quantify ways the models are biased. This is to avoid a common source of confusion: local methods can be used to derive aggregate statistics that characterize global properties of models. LIME (Ribeiro et al., 2016), for example, is mostly classified as a local method,[6] but in Ribeiro et al. (2016), the authors explicitly discuss how LIME can be used on i.i.d. samples to derive aggregate statistics that characterize model behavior on distributions. Definition 1.1 makes it clear that such methods are local; local methods *can* be applied globally, whereas global methods *cannot* be applied locally.

---

[6]Das and Rad (2020) classify it as *both* local and global.

It is also clear from Definition 1.1 that the two classes of interpretability methods are often motivated by different prototypical applications: local methods are often used to explain the motivation behind critical decisions, e.g., why a customer was assessed as high risk, why a traveling review was flagged as fraudulent, or why a newspaper article was flagged as misleading, whereas global methods are used to characterize biases in models and evaluate their robustness.

Challenge Definition 1.1 helps us clarify what we mean by local and global interpretability methods. Nevertheless, when applying this definition in practice, some methods can be a little harder to classify than others. Concept activation approaches, for example, use joint global training to learn mappings of individual examples into local explanations. Contrastive interpretability methods provide explanations in terms of pair of examples. Zhang et al. (2020) discuss what they call *semi-local* approaches, and Carvalho et al. (2019) introduce a category for interpretability methods that relate to groups of examples. It may also seem a bit unclear whether a challenge dataset provides a local or global explanation, for example.

Definition 1.1, however, focuses very clearly on the induction of explanations from representative samples. This focus leads us to classify concept activation methods as global, since the explanatory model component is induced from a representative sample (and relies, theoretically, on the representativity of this sample); we classify contrastive and group methods as local methods, since they do not assume representative samples; and, finally, we classify challenge datasets as local methods, since challenge datasets also do not have to be representative.

Examples Examples of *local* methods include gradients (Denil et al., 2014; Leray et al., 1998; Simonyan et al., 2014), layer-wise relevance propagation (Arras et al., 2016), deep Taylor decomposition (Montavon et al., 2017), integrated gradients (Mudrakarta et al., 2018; Sundararajan et al., 2017), DeepLift (Shrikumar et al., 2017), direct interpretation of gate or attention weights (Rei and Søgaard, 2018), attention roll-out and flow (Abnar and Zuidema, 2020), word association norms and analogies (Mikolov et al., 2013b), time step dynamics Strobelt et al. (2017), challenge datasets (Liu et al., 2019; Mullenbach et al., 2019; Richardson et al., 2013; Sun et al., 2019), local uptraining (Ribeiro et al., 2016), and influence sketching and influence functions (Koh and Liang, 2017); examples of *global* methods include unstructured pruning, lottery tickets, dynamic sparse training, binary networks, sparse coding, gate and attention head pruning, correlation of representations (Kriegeskorte et al., 2008), clustering (Aharoni and Goldberg, 2020; Trost and Klakow, 2017; Yenicelik et al., 2020), probing classifiers (Belinkov, 2021), concept activation (Kim et al., 2018), representer point selection (Yeh et al., 2018), TracIn (Pruthi et al., 2020a), and uptraining (Petrov et al., 2010).

1.1.2 INTRINSIC AND POST-HOC EXPLANATIONS

The distinction between intrinsic and post-hoc methods has many names, including *active-passive* in Zhang et al. (2020) and *self-explaining-ad hoc* in Danilevsky et al. (2020), all meant to introduce a distinction between *intrinsic* methods that jointly output explanations, and methods that derive these explanations *post-hoc* using techniques that are orthogonal to the models themselves. While most taxonomies introduce this distinction, we argue that it is inherently problematic.

Challenge   First of all, the distinction between intrinsic and post-hoc methods can be hard to maintain. Consider the difference between the two global interpretability methods, concept activation vectors and probing classifiers: CAV are trained jointly, probing classifiers sequentially. These are extremes of a (curriculum) continuum, which is hard to binarize: if a probing classifier is trained jointly with the last epoch of the model training, is the method then intrinsic or post-hoc? For a real example, consider TracIn (Pruthi et al., 2020a), in which influence functions are estimated across various training check points. Again, is TracIn intrinsic or post-hoc? That the binary distinction covers a continuum, makes the distinction hard to apply in practice. Moreover, for a method to be *post-hoc* means different things to local and global methods. A post-hoc, local method is post-hoc relative to a class inference (in the case of classification); a post-hoc, global method is post-hoc relative to training, introducing a disjoint training phase for learning the interpretability functions. Strictly speaking, the fact that "post-hoc" takes on two disjoint meanings for local and global methods, namely *post-inference* and *post-training*, makes taxonomies that rely on both dimensions inconsistent.

1.2   SHORTCOMINGS OF EXISTING TAXONOMIES

We have seen that the intrinsic-post-hoc distinction found in most taxonomies is inconsistent. We now briefly, yet critically, assess the 10 taxonomies, pointing out the ways in which they are inconsistent, incomplete, or redundant.

1.2.1   GUIDOTTI ET AL. (2018)

Guidotti et al. (2018) first introduce the distinction between local and global interpretability methods, as well as two that relate to how explanations are communicated (how much time the user is expected to have to understand the model decisions, and how much domain knowledge and technical experience the user is expected to have). In addition to the terms *local* and *global*, they also refer, synonymously, to *outcome explanation* and *model explanation*. Later in their survey, Guidotti et al. (2018) make a fourth distinction that is very similar to intrinsic-post-hoc, namely between *transparent design* (leading to intrinsically interpretable models) and (post-hoc) *black box inspection*, but oddly, this is not seen as an orthogonal dimension, but as two additional classes *on par* with outcome and model explanation.

Challenge   How to classify methods that are *both*, say, local and post-hoc, i.e., do outcome explanation by black-box inspection? Examples would include gradients (Denil et al., 2014; Leray et al., 1998; Simonyan et al., 2014), layer-wise relevance propagation (Arras et al., 2016), deep Taylor decomposition (Montavon et al., 2017), integrated gradients (Mudrakarta et al., 2018; Sundararajan et al., 2017), etc.

1.2.2   ADADI AND BERRADA (2019)

Adadi and Berrada (2018) rely on the local-global and intrinsic-post-hoc distinctions (referring to the later as *complexity*), and, as a third dimension, they distinguish between model-agnostic and model-specific interpretability methods.

Inconsistencies   We argue that the distinction between model-specific and model-agnostic methods is suboptimal in that state-of-the-art models are moving targets, and so is what counts as model-specific. This may lead to inconsistencies over time.

Challenge   How do we classify a method that applies to all known methods, but not to all possible methods?

1.2.3   CARVALHO ET AL. (2019)

Carvalho et al. (2019) introduce four dimensions in their taxonomy: (a) *scope*, which coincides with the local-global distinction (Definition 1.1); (b) *intrinsic-post-hoc*; (c) *pre-model, in-model, and post-model*, with *in-model* corresponding to intrinsic methods, and *post-model* corresponding to post-hoc methods, whereas *pre-model* comprises various approaches to data analysis. We argue below that (c) is both redundant and inconsistent. Finally, they introduce (d) a *results* dimension, which concerns the *form* of the explanations provided by the methods. We discuss this (somewhat orthogonal) aspect of interpretability methods in §1.3.

Inconsistencies   In addition to the inconsistency of intrinsic-post-hoc, including pre-model explanations leads to further taxonomic inconsistency in that pre-model approaches cannot be classified along the other dimensions in that they do not refer to models at all. For the same reason, one might argue they are not model interpretation methods in the first place.

Redundancies   The redundancy of (c) follows from the observation that the distinction between in-model and post-model explanations is identical to the distinction made in (b), as well as the observation that pre-model explanations do not refer to models at all[7].

Challenge   What is an intrinsic interpretability method that presents post-model explanations, or a post-hoc interpretability method that presents in-model explanations?

---

[7]In other words, all in-model explanations are intrinsic, and all post-model explanations are post-hoc. Carvalho et al. (2019) are explicit about this redundancy: "In-model interpretability concerns ML models that have inherent interpretability in it (through constraints or not), being intrinsically interpretable. Post-model interpretability refers to improving interpretability after building a model (post hoc)".

1.2.4   MOLNAR (2019)

Molnar (2019) also distinguishes between local-global and intrinsic-post-hoc, as well as between different *results*. Their taxonomy thus relies on three out of four of the dimensions in Carvalho et al. (2019); instead of the distinction between pre-model, in-model and post-model explanations, they instead distinguish between model-specific and model-agnostic methods.

Inconsistencies   See the discussion of Adadi and Berrada (2018), which also applies here. In addition, the results dimension distinguishes between intrinsic interpretations and feature summary statistics is also inconsistent in that explanations can, simultaneously, be intrinsically interpretable models and feature summary statistics. LIME (Ribeiro et al., 2016), for example, presents local explanations as the linear coefficients of a linear fit, i.e., an intrinsically interpretable model that consists solely of feature summary statistics.

Redundancies   The most important redundancy in the taxonomy presented in Molnar (2019) is that all model-agnostic interpretability methods are also post-hoc, since intrinsic methods require joint training, which in turn requires compatibility with model architectures. Moreover, model-agnostic interpretability methods are all grounded in input features and thus lead to explanations in terms of feature summary statistics or visualizations. Moreover, all explanations in terms of intrinsically interpretable models are, quite obviously, intrinsic.

Challenge   What is a post-hoc interpretability method whose explanations are intrinsically interpretable models?

1.2.5   ZHANG ET AL. (2020)

Zhang et al. (2020) present a three-dimensional taxonomy with the following dimensions: (a) global-local; (b) intrinsic-post-hoc (which they call *active-passive*; and (c) a distinction between four *explanation types*, namely *examples*, *attribution*, *hidden semantics*, and *rules*.

Inconsistencies   The *explanation type* dimension in Zhang et al. (2020) conflates two different things, namely the model components we are trying to explain, and what the explanations look like. Hidden semantics, for example, is a model component, whereas examples and rules refer (somewhat vaguely) to the (syntactic) *form* of the explanations. The distinction between hidden semantics and attribution, for example, is also apparent. Hidden semantics can be used to *derive* attribution (a results type in Carvalho et al. (2019) and Molnar (2019)), e.g., in LSTMVis, the visualization software presented by Strobelt et al. (2017); this is because hidden semantics is not a type of explanation, but a model component. Attribution, examples, and rules *are* types of explanations, but this list is not exhaustive, since explanations can also be in terms of concepts, free texts, or visualizations, for example.

Challenge   What is a passive interpretability method that does not provide local explanations?[8]

[8]Inherently interpretable models are not *methods*, but simply models that are directly interpretable.

1.2.6 DANILEVSKY ET AL. (2020)

Danilevsky et al. (2020) present a two-dimensional taxonomy, distinguishing only between global-local and intrinsic-post-hoc (which they call *self-explaining* and *ad-hoc*) methods.

Inconsistencies   Danilevsky et al. (2020) cite a lot of attribution methods as global and ad-hoc. We wish to argue that such attribution methods are necessarily local, and while aggregate statistics can of course be computed across real or synthetic corpora, little is gained by blurring taxonomies to reflect that. All local methods can be used to compute summary statistics; this is completely orthogonal to any differences between these methods. This inconsistency follows from the their definition of local-global (see §1.1.1).

Incompleteness   Danilevsky et al. (2020) admit their survey is biased toward local methods, and many global interpretability methods are left uncovered.[9]

Challenge   What is a local interpretability method that cannot be used to compute summary statistics?

1.2.7 DAS ET AL. (2020)

Das and Rad (2020) present a three-way taxonomy. They also distinguish between local and global methods. Their second dimension is called *methodology*, in which they distinguish between methods based on back-propagation or gradient-based methods on the one hand–and perturbation-based methods on the other; their third dimension is called *usage*, in which they distinguish between intrinsic and post-hoc methods. As is evident from their classification of current approaches, their taxonomy is both *incomplete* and *redundant*.

Incompleteness   Several approaches are neither gradient-based or perturbation-based.

Redundancies   All gradient-based approaches are classified as post-hoc approaches in Das and Rad (2020); similarly, all intrinsic methods are classified as global methods. Of course these cells may be filled with methods that were not covered, but in particular, it seems that gradient-based approaches are, almost always, post-hoc?[10]

Challenge   What is an intrinsic, gradient-based approach?

---

[9]The only example they cite for the class of global and self-explaining methods is Pröllochs et al. (2019), a paper on using reinforcement learning to learn interpretable rules. The method in Pröllochs et al. (2019) learns a global policy to extract these rules. See §1.1.1 for a list of methods left uncovered.

[10]Weight pruning methods that rely on gradients seem like a counter example, but typically, gradients are only used to prune weights *after* a full round of training, and these methods are therefore best seen as *post-hoc* methods.

1.2.8   ATANASOVA ET AL. (2020)

Atanasova et al. (2020a) distinguish between three classes of explainability methods: gradient-based, perturbation-based, and simplification-based methods, evaluating examples of each across various NLP tasks.

Inconsistencies   The distinction between gradient-based and perturbation-based methods is similar to Das and Rad (2020), but the two classifications are inconsistent, with Atanasova et al. (2020a) citing LIME Ribeiro et al. (2016) as a simplification-based method. It seems that the distinction between perturbation-based and simplification-based methods is in itself inconsistent in that both perturbations and gradients can be used to simplify models; similarly, perturbations can be used to baseline gradient-based approaches.

Incompleteness   Clearly, not all interpretability methods are gradient-based, perturbation-based or simplification-based: other methods are based on weight magnitudes, carefully designed example templates, visualizing and quantifying attention weights or gating mechanisms.

Challenge   How would you classify attention roll-out Abnar and Zuidema (2020), for example?

1.2.9   KOTONYA AND TONI (2020)

Kotonya and Toni (2020) distinguish between attention-based explanations, explanations as rule discovery, and explanations as summarization.

Incompleteness   Several things are not easily fitted into this classification scheme. Using gating mechanisms to interpret models, for example, does not seem to fit any of the three categories.

Inconsistencies   This classification defines one class of interpretability methods in terms of the model components being interpreted (attention-based) and another in terms of the *form* of explanations they provide (rule discovery and summarization). Mixing orthogonal dimensions is inconsistent, since methods easily can belong to several categories, e.g., attention head pruning (Voita et al., 2019), which is both attention-based and a form of summarization, or when rules are induced from attention weights (Ruzsics et al., 2021).

Chen et al. (2021)   Chen et al. (2021) introduce the global-local distinction, but not the intrinsic-post-hoc distinction. In addition, they distinguish between interpretability methods that present explanations in terms of training instances, approximations, feature attribution, and counterfactuals.

Inconsistencies   The second dimension again makes orthogonal distinctions. Approximations, for example, can be used to attribute importance to features (LIME).

Incompleteness   Explanations in terms of concepts, attention weights, gate activations, rules, etc., are not covered by the second dimension.

Redundancies   All methods that present explanations in terms of training instances are necessarily local.

Challenge   What's a global interpretability method providing explanations in terms of training instances?

1.3   THE METHOD-FORM FALLACY

Several of the above taxonomies include dimensions that pertain to the (syntactic) form of the output of interpretation methods. We argue such distinctions are completely orthogonal to the interpretability methods and should therefore not be included in taxonomies. To see this, note that most interpretability methods, e.g., LIME, can provide explanations of different form: aggregate statistics, coefficients, rules, visualizations, etc.[11]

1.4   INCONSISTENT CLASSIFICATIONS

Figure 1.1a shows that taxonomies are not only internally inconsistent, but also inconsistent (between them) in how they classify methods. Somewhat surprisingly, only six interpretability methods were mentioned by more than one of the above surveys; since the taxonomies rely on the same two dimensions (global-local and intrinsic-post-hoc), we can easily compare whether these six methods are classified consistently. For those six methods, only two were classified consistently by different surveys. Four in six methods were classified differently. Concept activation (§8.4), for example, is classified as intrinsic in Molnar (2019), but as post-hoc in Zhang et al. (2020).[12]

1.5   A NOVEL TAXONOMY

Our proposed taxonomy is quite simple and contains only two dimensions. One is local-global, like other taxonomies, and the other is a distinction between explanations based on *forward*

---

[11]That said, many observations can be made about the syntactic form of explanations. All methods that return extractive rationales, for example, suffer from the following *inherent* limitations: (i) these methods can only explain decisions in terms of tokens or features *present* in the input, but not in terms of tokens or features *absent* from the input (Dhurandhar et al., 2018); (ii) sometimes explanations are not about the presence or absence of input tokens or features, but about how they relate, or add up. To see (i), think of how explaining why good sentiment models label some sentences as *neutral*, for example, is more about the absence of polarity words than about the presence of any other words. Limitation (ii) shows up, for example, when explaining the decisions of a model trained to detect sentences with more digits and punctuation than letters. Such a model would pay equal attention to all characters in a sentence, and a highlighting of the most important tokens or features would not really provide us with *any* explanation of the inner workings of the model. In our taxonomy, this limitation primarily concerns local backward methods (see Observation 5.1).

[12]We classify concept activation as *global-forward*.

passes through neural networks and explanations based on *backward* passes. Note that a backward pass can accumulate not only gradients, but also relevance scores (Arras et al., 2016), for example. The forward explanations typically correlate intermediate representations or continuous or discrete output representations to obtain explanations, whereas backward explanations concern the training dynamics. We define the distinction between forward and backward methods in the following way.

Definition 1.2   Forward-backward.   An interpretability method is said to be *backward* if it relies solely on quantities derived from one or more backward passes through the instances; otherwise, if it relies on quantities from forward passes, it is said to be *forward*.

Local backward methods include gradients (Denil et al., 2014; Leray et al., 1998; Simonyan et al., 2014), integrated gradients (Mudrakarta et al., 2018; Sundararajan et al., 2017), layer-wise relevance propagation (Bach et al., 2015), DeepLIFT (Shrikumar et al., 2017), and deep Taylor decomposition (Montavon et al., 2017), which all derive explanations for individual instances from what is normally used as training signals, typically based on derivatives of the loss function (gradients) evaluating h on training data, e.g., $d(\ell(h(\mathbf{x}_i), y_i))$. Global backward methods rely on such training signals to modify or extend the model parameters $\mathbf{w}$ associated with h, typically extracting approximations, rules, or visualizations.

Local forward methods either consider intermediate representations, e.g., gates (Lakretz et al., 2019), attention (Rei and Søgaard, 2018), attention flow (Abnar and Zuidema, 2020), etc.; continuous output representations, e.g., using word association norms (Church and Hanks, 1989) or word analogies (Garneau et al., 2021; Mikolov et al., 2013a); or discrete output, such as when evaluating on challenge datasets (Liu et al., 2019; Mullenbach et al., 2019; Richardson et al., 2013; Sun et al., 2019), or when approximating the model's output distribution (Alvarez-Melis and Jaakkola, 2017; Koh and Liang, 2017; Ribeiro et al., 2016). In the same way, global forward methods can rely on intermediate representations in forward passes, e.g., in attention head pruning (Voita et al., 2019), attention factor analysis (Kobayashi et al., 2020), syntactic decoding of attention heads (Ravishankar et al., 2021), attention head manipulation (Vashishth et al., 2019), etc.; continuous output in forward passes, including work using clustering in the vector space to manually analyze model representations (Heylen et al., 2012; Reif et al., 2019), probing classifiers (Belinkov, 2021), and concept activation strategies (Kim et al., 2018); or on discrete output, e.g., in uptraining (Petrov et al., 2010) and knowledge distillation (Kim and Rush, 2016).

CHAPTER 2

A Framework for Explainable NLP

An NLP model is a hypothesis $h(\cdot)$ from some hypothesis class $\mathcal{H}$. In the early days of NLP, h was selected or designed by hand, but today, h is typically induced from a sample of n data points $D = \{\langle \mathbf{x}_i, y_i \rangle \mid i \leq n\}$ by a learning algorithm. In linear classification, $\mathcal{H}$ is the set of all possible lines (hyperplanes), and the perceptron learning algorithm, for example, can be used to search for a good line $h(\cdot)$ by iteratively correcting the errors made by the current hypothesis. Other popular model classes in NLP include recurrent neural networks and transformers. It is the decisions of such learned models we wish to *explain*. This chapter first introduces standard architectures in NLP that, in combination with task-specific input and output spaces, will define the hypothesis classes from which $h(\cdot)$ will be induced. Once we have been reminded about these standard architectures, we are in a position to introduce a simple, yet incredibly useful, framework for thinking about interpretability methods.

2.1 NLP ARCHITECTURES

2.1.1 LINEAR AND NONLINEAR CLASSIFICATION

A linear model is a parameter vector $\mathbf{w}$ that interacts with a data point $\mathbf{x}$ in the following way to produce a class prediction y:

$$y = b \times 1 + w_0 x_0 + w_1 x_1 + w_2 x_2 + \ldots = \mathbf{w}\mathbf{x}^T$$

The decision of a linear model is the sign of the inner-product of model parameters and the representation (vectorization) of the data instance. Our learning algorithms will attempt to select $\mathbf{w}$ such as to minimize our loss across D, $\ell(h(\mathbf{x}_i), y_i)$. We will assume a smooth, differentiable loss function, e.g., logistic loss, $-y_i \log(h(\mathbf{x}_i))$. Saliency maps (Fong et al., 2019) are a broad class of explanation methods that analyze how a change in some input $\mathbf{x}$ changes the output y. A straightforward way to do this in the case of linear classification models is to take the derivative of the loss function with respect to the input, $d(\ell(h(\mathbf{x}_i), y_i))$. We discuss saliency maps in more detail in Chapter 3.

Nonlinear classification models, like linear ones, come in many different flavors, but the vast majority of recent research in NLP revolves around recurrent models and transformers.

2.1.2 RECURRENT MODELS

A simple vanilla recurrent neural network for sequences of variable length n is a multi-layered perceptron with n tied layers, i.e., a variable set of layers with the same parameter weights. The n tied layers are used to process a sequence of n time steps, represented by vectors (embeddings) $t_1 \ldots t_n$. Formally, the hidden representation at time step t_i is $h_{t_i} = \sigma(\mathbf{w}^e \mathbf{x}_{t_i} + \mathbf{w} h_{t_{i-1}})$ with $\mathbf{x}_{t_i}$ the one-hot vector encoding token t_i, and where $\mathbf{w}^e$ is a separate set of model parameters commonly referred to as the *embedding layer*.

The advantage of recurrent networks is that they condition the representation of each sequence token on the representation of its left context. It is common to design bidirectional architectures that enable conditioning on both left and right context by simply concatenating the representations of two recurrent networks, processing the input in opposite order.

In practice, most researchers rely on *gated recurrent networks*. We briefly discuss these, since gates are intermediate representations that have been used to explain the decisions of recurrent networks. Several gating techniques exist, but in NLP, two techniques have gained the most traction: gated recurrent units (GRUs) (Cho et al., 2014) and long short-term memory cells (Hochreiter and Schmidhuber, 1997).

GRUs The key difference between a simple recurrent network and a network with GRUs is that the model parameters (including the embedding layer) are split (or copied) in three independent sets of parameters, $\mathbf{w}, \mathbf{w}^z, \mathbf{w}^r$. We first compute what is commonly referred to as the update gate vector z_{t_i}:

$$z_{t_i} = \sigma_z(\mathbf{w}_z^e \mathbf{x}_{t_i} + \mathbf{w}_z h_{t_{i-1}})$$

Intuitively, the update gate vector controls which weights are updates in the current time step. Next we compute the reset gate vector, which is used to ensure memory flow throughout the sequence:

$$r_{t_i} = \sigma_r(\mathbf{w}_r^e \mathbf{x}_{t_i} + \mathbf{w}_r h_{t_{i-1}})$$

Note that both these update rules are identical to the update rule in simple recurrent networks. With those two vectors, we can now compute our hidden state representations in two steps. First, we compute

$$\hat{h}_{t_i} = \sigma(\mathbf{w}^e \mathbf{x}_{t_i} + \mathbf{w}(r_{t_i} \circ h_{t_{i-1}}))$$

which is the standard update rule after factoring in the reset gate vector, controlling the information flow from the previous state $h_{t_{i-1}}$. Second, we compute

$$h_{t_i} = (1 - z_{t-i}) \circ h_{t_{i-1}} + z_t \circ \hat{h}_{t_i}$$

which intuitively uses the update gate vector to focus on parts of the current time step and demote the corresponding part of the previous time step. In other words, the update gate vector is used to control the relative importance of the current input over the context. Many researchers have been interested in the extent to which recurrent networks rely on context (Weiss et al., 2018), which makes update gate vector weights an interesting object of analysis.

LSTMs   Just like GRUs divide the weights into three and apply three independent updates (per layer) in every time step, LSTMs divide the weights into four subspaces: the basic weights ($\mathbf{w}$), the input weights ($\mathbf{w}^i$), the output weights ($\mathbf{w}^o$), and the forget gates ($\mathbf{w}^f$). We compute the input and output activation vectors, i_{t_i} and o_{t_i}, as well as the forget gate activation vector, f_{t_i}, with the standard update rules, applied to the relevant parameters. We now compute *two* intermediate time step representations; $\hat{c}_{t_i}$ is computed using the standard update rule (just like $\hat{h}_{t_i}$ in GRUs). We then compute

$$c_{t_i} = f_{t_i} \circ c_{t_{i-1}} + i_{t_i} \circ \hat{c}_{t_i}$$

and finally set h_{t_i} to $o_{t_i} \circ \sigma(c_{t_i})$. The input, output, and forget gates have all been objects of interpretation (Lakretz et al., 2019).

For more details on recurrent networks, we refer the interested reader to another book in this book series, Goldberg (2017).

2.1.3   TRANSFORMERS

The Transformer architecture (Vaswani et al., 2017) constrains a soft alignment (self-attention) to be learned across discrete states in the input. Just like recurrent networks maintain hidden states to draw on context information, transformers rely on self-attention to capture long-distance dependencies. We obtain self-attention by maintaining several vectors using distinct sets of model parameters, $\mathbf{w}^q$ (for query vectors), $\mathbf{w}^k$ (for key vectors), and $\mathbf{w}^v$ (for value vectors). Multiplying the embedding vector[1] for a particular time step with $\mathbf{w}^q$ gives us the query vector for that time step, etc. The self-attention across the input tokens $t_1 \dots t_n$ associated with a particular time step t_i is obtained by computing the dot products of t_i's query vector $\mathbf{w}^q \mathbf{x}_{t_i}$ with the key vectors of the other words, subsequently passing these values through a softmax operator. We then integrate context information accordingly by multiplying the softmax values into the value vectors of these words. The sum of these weighted value vectors is the self-attention presentation for the time step t_i. In practice, we typically use multiple sets of query, key, and value vectors, often referred to as *attention heads*. Attention heads are the object of interpretation in both local and global interpretability methods, e.g., using attention flow (Abnar and Zuidema, 2020) or attention head pruning (Voita et al., 2019). To produce the final output, the output

---

[1]One advantage of transformers is that we can do inference for input tokens in parallel, but at the expense of word order infromation. As a hack, the embedding vectors are combined with so-called *positional embeddings* to encode word order information; this hack makes sense for monolingual language models, but known failure modes in the context of multilingual language models (Dufter and Schütze, 2020; Liu et al., 2020).

of the transformer multi-head self-attention architecture is added to its input, normalized and passed through feed-forward layers.

2.1.4   OVERVIEW OF APPLICATIONS AND ARCHITECTURES

Word embeddings and language models   Language models traditionally served the purpose of ranking more or less likely sentences. When word embeddings were first introduced, however, it was with a different purpose in mind, namely learning representations of words that enable lexical generalization (Turian et al., 2010). Modern language models now serve both purposes (Khandelwal et al., 2020): they provide representations that generalize and enable similarity judgments, and can be used to rank more or less likely sentences. Word embeddings are typically learned using linear or nonlinear classification algorithms, but can also be side products of language models based on recurrent or transformer architectures.

Sentiment analysis and related applications   A large chunk of NLP is concerned with document classification problems such as sentiment analysis, fake news detection, argument mining, and so on. Historically, these tasks have been modeled with linear and nonlinear classification algorithms, possibly relying on word embeddings, but these days, most algorithms rely on representations learned with recurrent or transformer architectures.

Inference and related applications   A wide range of other tasks can be construed as classification of pairs of sentences or chunks of texts, including natural language inference, question answering, stance detection, etc. For these tasks, we can generally use the same methods as for document classification tasks.

Syntactic and semantic parsers   For a handful of traditional NLP tasks, the input is a sentence, and the output is a tree or directed acyclic graph representing a linguistic analysis. We will ignore the complexities of structured prediction with graphs in this book, i.e., the search algorithms used to find optimal subgraphs in weight matrices, but refer the interested reader to another book in this book series, Kubler et al. (2009). We will, however, refer to core concepts in syntactic and semantic parsing, as well as to the linguistic knowledge these models are designed to capture.

Translation models   Translation models generally consist of two parts: an encoder and a decoder. We will not discuss these in any detail, but simply note that the two most prominent architectures are based on recurrent and transformer architectures. A recurrent encoder-decoder architecture was first introduced in Sutskever et al. (2014) and generally consists of a recurrent encoder that encodes the input sentence. The decoder then generates a string from the input encoding, predicting one token at a time (like a language model). This architecture became competitive with existing translation models at the time, when combined the recurrent architecture with attention, enabling generation from a (dynamically) weighted mixture of hidden states associated with input time steps, rather than simply from a vector encoding the entire input sentence. Transformer architectures can be used in encoder-decoder architectures in the same way.

2.2   LOCAL AND GLOBAL EXPLANATIONS

In the rest of the book, we rely on the two-dimensional taxonomy presented in Chapter 1, distinguishing between *local* and *global* interpretability methods, as well as between *forward* and *backward* ones. To add additional structure to the book, and to balance the chapters a bit, we further distinguish between forward methods that focus on intermediate representations, continuous output, or discontinuous output. This is not a clear-cut, taxonomical distinction, and it is easy to imagine methods that focus equally on all three modes of representation, but we found it helpful to group interpretability methods this way.

This way we end up with eight categories of interpretability methods, four local and four global ones: Recall how local methods are typically motivated by an interest in explaining the inner workings of h leading to critical decisions (on that small set of examples of specific interest), e.g., *why* a traveling review was flagged as fraudulent, or a newspaper article flagged as misleading. These methods are designed to explain local decisions or decision boundaries and are used, for example, when an insurance customer needs to know why they were estimated to be high risk customers. The customer is not interested in the global properties of the model, only why *they* were labeled high-risk, regardless of how representative they were of the underlying population. Global methods, in contrast, are typically motivated by an interested in the **global** properties of h, e.g., whether h is sparse, biased, unfair, or subscribes to particular beliefs. Such methods are used to evaluate models, identify their vulnerabilities, estimate their sensitivity to drift, etc. Both local and global methods can rely on backward or forward passes through the neural networks they seek to explain. This leads to four categories, as discussed in Chapter 1.

We now further sub-divide the class of local-forward methods into local methods that explain models locally by forward passing weights to form (a) intermediate representations, (b) continuous output, or (c) discrete output; and global methods into global methods that explain models globally in the same way. This, in total, leads to eight categories. The eight categories are described in the next eight chapters, Chapters 3–10.

2.3   BACKWARD METHODS

Backward methods rely on signals that are passed backward through neural networks, e.g., backpropagated error gradients or relevance scores. Chapters 3 and 4 cover explanation methods that derive explanations from training signals, typically based on derivatives of the loss function (gradients) evaluating h on training data, e.g., $d(\ell(h(\mathbf{x}_i), y_i))$. Chapter 3 deals with local methods that do not require learning of additional parameters, but provide *direct* interpretations of single examples based on model gradients. We begin with simple approaches that rely on vanilla gradients to construct saliency maps and proceed with more sophisticated techniques, including integrated gradients (Mudrakarta et al., 2018; Sundararajan et al., 2017), layer-wise relevance propagation (Bach et al., 2015), DeepLIFT (Shrikumar et al., 2017), deep Taylor decomposition (Montavon et al., 2017), as well as their applications in NLP. In Chapter 4, we then proceed with methods that rely on training signals (gradients or resulting weight magnitudes) to extract smaller, approximate characterizations of models. Most of these methods require additional training on a representative sample of data, e.g., lottery tickets (Frankle and Carbin, 2019; Movva and Zhao, 2020) and will either modify or extend the model parameters **w** associated with h.

2.4 FORWARD EXPLAINING BY INTERMEDIATE REPRESENTATIONS

For brevity, we simply refer to explanations by forward passes to form intermediate representations as explanations by or of intermediate representations. Some architectures rely on intermediate representations during inference that can also be the object of explanations. One example of this is *gates* in recurrent architectures. Gates were, for example, used to explain model decisions in Lakretz et al. (2019). More recently, many researchers have explored *attention* in recurrent and transformer architectures. This is today one of the most popular approaches to explaining neural network decisions. Most of this work focuses on *directly* explaining model decisions on specific data points (local decisions), without training, but there is also a significant body of work on using additional training to characterize the global, structural properties of attention heads in trained models (Ravishankar et al., 2021). In Chapter 5, we discuss the following local explainability methods: gates (Lakretz et al., 2019), attention (Rei and Søgaard, 2018), attention flow (Abnar and Zuidema, 2020), etc.; in Chapter 6, we discuss global explainability methods for intermediate representations, including attention head pruning (Voita et al., 2019), attention factor analysis (Kobayashi et al., 2020), syntactic decoding of attention heads Ravishankar et al. (2021), attention head manipulation (Vashishth et al., 2019), etc.

In the taxonomy presented here, the least motivated distinction, in my view, is that between what I call intermediate representations and what I call training dynamics. Gates and attention weights are really just weights, like the weights of a feed-forward layer, and in a way, there is no obvious reason to distinguish between approaches to explainable NLP that focus on gates and attention weights, and approaches that focus on weights and gradients in general. However, since gates and attention weights have been a locus of research in explainable NLP, I have introduced the distinction nevertheless, to make the representation below as coherent as possible, and to divide the burden between the various chapters more equally.

2.5   FORWARD EXPLAINING BY CONTINUOUS OUTPUTS

Deep neural networks—whether they are feed-forward, recurrent, or transformer architectures—are representation learning devices. Or, in other words, they are (in our case, language) *encoders*. While they output class labels, or sequences of tags or output symbols, they also provide vector representations of the input, which can be used for multiple purposes. Imagine a feed-forward network accepting bag-of-word representations of documents as input, passing information through a densely connected hidden layer of d weights, and then to a logistic regression classifier, trained on data for a document classification task. The hidden layer provides a d-dimensional representation that supposedly better represents the aspects of documents relevant for the task at hand. If you throw away the classifier, we are left with a mapping from bag-of-word representations to d-dimensional document embeddings that may also be useful for related tasks. This observation, and the vision of all-purpose representations, is what has driven the resurgent interest in multi-task learning with deep architectures (Baxter, 2000; Caruana, 1993; Søgaard and Goldberg, 2016).

Such embeddings can be learned for characters, words, phrases, and documents. Direct interpretations of vector representations of words, for example, include using word association norms to query for whether nearest neighbors in vector space align with human intuitions (Church and Hanks, 1989). Other work uses word analogies (Garneau et al., 2021; Mikolov et al., 2013a) to test whether the vector space is well-structured. Chapter 7 covers the above. Finally, Chapter 8 covers representational similarity analysis (Kriegeskorte et al., 2008), which was originally used to analyze fMRI encodings, but has recently become a popular technique for comparing vector spaces, as well as a range of other global techniques for explaining NLP models at the level of their representations or continuous output, including work using clustering in the vector space to manually analyze model representations (Heylen et al., 2012; Reif et al., 2019), probing classifiers Belinkov (2021), and concept activation strategies Kim et al. (2018).

2.6   FORWARD EXPLAINING BY DISCRETE OUTPUTS

The architectures discussed in this book also produce discrete outputs, y_i, of course, ranging from class labels to words and to sequences of words (sentences). Some of the work on explaining architectures by looking at their (discrete) output resembles traditional error analysis. This holds for many recent papers on challenge datasets (Liu et al., 2019; Mullenbach et al., 2019; Richardson et al., 2013; Sun et al., 2019), for example. Here, architectures are analyzed or explained by looking at their performance on interesting edge cases collected in carefully constructed test suites. Challenge datasets are examples of local explanations by discrete outputs and are discussed in Chapter 9. Challenge datasets can be combined with surprisal studies (Ettinger, 2020). **Other examples covered in Chapter** 9 **include LIME** (Ribeiro et al., 2016), **causal analysis** (Alvarez-Melis and Jaakkola, 2017), **and influence functions** (Koh and Liang, 2017).

Chapter 10 **covers global interpretations of discrete output. If the model complexity of** h **prevents direct explanation by inspecting its parameters, a common technique is to first learn a more interpretable approximation of** h. **For example, by learning a linear approximation of a deep neural network, we can directly inspect the interaction of the coefficients of the linear model and input features to (approximately**[2]**) explain the decisions of the network we learned to approximate. I briefly review the most common ways of learning such approximations, including uptraining** (Petrov et al., 2010) **and knowledge distillation** (Kim and Rush, 2016). **The chapter also covers self-explained neural networks, trained with the auxiliary objective of generating explanations** (Narang et al., 2020).

---

[2]Needless to say, approximation can be very misleading at times.

CHAPTER 3

Local-Backward Explanations

This chapter captures explanation methods that use training signals or training dynamics to directly explain model decisions. The explanations are *direct*, in the sense that they do not require induction of additional parameters, and *local*, in that the explanations do not aim to generalize across representative samples of data: each data point is explained on its own terms.

3.1 VANILLA GRADIENTS

The seminal method within this class is simply using vanilla gradients to explain a model decision. Early work on using gradients for explainable NLP goes (at least) back to 2014 (Denil et al., 2014; Simonyan et al., 2014), but the method itself is even older (Leray et al., 1998).

The key intuition is to compute the gradient of the loss function or the logit of the predicted class with respect to the input embeddings given model parameters[1]

$$\frac{d(\ell(h(\mathbf{x}_i), y_i))}{d(\mathbf{w})}$$

by simply running regular gradient back-propagation without changing weights. You can do this on a single data point (to derive an explanation) or on a validation dataset (to do feature selection or weight pruning). Since the method works on a single data point, this is classified as a *local* method that relies on training dynamics (gradients).

3.2 GUIDED BACK-PROPAGATION

The machine learning literature is rich on small, incremental improvements over using vanilla gradients, and I include guided back-propagation (Springenberg et al., 2015) to illustrate this. The common idea behind using vanilla gradients and guided back-propagation is to compute the gradient of the network's prediction with respect to the input, holding the weights fixed. This determines which input elements need to be changed the least to affect the prediction the most. While using vanilla gradients relies on actual gradients, guided back-propagation only back-propagates positive error signals, setting negative gradients to zero, reflecting the intuition that positive gradients provide more direct explanations of model decisions. While Atanasova et al. (2020a) evaluate guided back-propagation across a range of NLP tasks, the method was

---

[1]We cannot compute the gradient with respect to tokens, only with respect to their embeddings. We therefore must reduce the d-dimensional gradients to a scalar value, e.g., by computing their ℓ_n norm.

Method	Year	Reference
Vanilla gradients	2014	Denil et al. (2014)
Guided back-propagation	2015	Springenberg et al. (2015)
Layer-wise relevance propagation	2015	Bach et al. (2015)
Deep Taylor decomposition	2017	Montavon et al. (2017)
Integrated gradients	2017	Sundararajan et al. (2017)
DeepLift	2017	Shrikumar et al. (2017)

Figure 3.1: Methods: Local Explanations of Training Dynamics.

developed for computer vision applications of convolutional neural networks, and it is not immediately obvious that guided back-propagation is motivated for standard NLP tasks.

3.3   LAYER-WISE RELEVANCE PROPAGATION

Layer-wise relevance propagation replace standard back-propagation with carefully designed back-propagation rules for relevance values. To see what this involves, let j and k be weights at consecutive layers. The relevance propagation from all such weights k to j

$$R_j = \sum_k \frac{a_j \mathbf{w}_{jk}}{\sum_j a_j \mathbf{w}_{jk}} R_k$$

is the normalized product of the activation of j and the model parameter connecting j and k, i.e., intuitively, the relative contribution of j toward making k relevant. The method back-propagates relevance recursively from the output layer to the input layer in this way. We can obtain sparser explanations by adding an ϵ to the denominator in the above. A major advantage of this method compared to the above is that it does not require neural activations to be smooth or differentiable. Layer-wise relevance propagation can be seen as an instance of deep Taylor expansion (Montavon et al., 2017), and if $\epsilon = 0$, it is equivalent to a restricted version of DeepLift (Kindermans et al., 2016); both are discussed below.

Layer-wise relevance propagation is widely used in NLP. Arras et al. (2016) were first to use it for document classification using convolutional networks. Arras et al. (2017) then used it to explain the decisions of sentiment analysis systems based on recurrent architectures. Ding et al. (2017) used the method for explaining recurrent architectures for neural machine translation. Poerner et al. (2018) compared layer-wise relevance propagation to other local, gradient-based methods for the tasks of question answering and morpho-syntactic agreement. Arras et al. (2019) compared layer-wise relevance propagation with vanilla gradients, integrated gradients, and occlusion (Chapter 9), as well as a technique specifically developed for recurrent networks. They argue that the variant of layer-wise relevance propagation introduced in Arras et al. (2017) is superior to all these other methods. Voita et al. (2019) propose using layer-wise relevance propagation to identify transformer attention heads that can be pruned; see Chapter 6 for a discussion of attention head pruning in transformer architectures. Calvillo and Crocker (2018), in contrast, use layer-wise relevance propagation to compute corpus-wide (aggregate) word statistics and analyze differences between different morphosyntactic and semantic word classes.

3.4   DEEP TAYLOR DECOMPOSITION

Deep Taylor decomposition (Montavon et al., 2017) applies Taylor decomposition on the local relevance functions of R_j in order to redistribute relevances to lower layers. This instantiates the hyperparameters of layer-wise relevance propagation, including ϵ, previously set heuristically. The only variable is the root point $\mathbf{x_0}$ at which the Taylor expansion is performed. Montavon et al. (2017) present a few methods for selecting good root points (that remove an object of interest, but deviate only slightly from $\mathbf{x_i}$). The final feature importance map is the element-wise product between the gradient of $\frac{df}{d\mathbf{x_i}}$, the root point $\mathbf{x_0}$, with f the Taylor expansion, and the difference $\mathbf{x_i} - \mathbf{x_0}$. Schwarzenberg et al. (2019a) and Chefer et al. (2020) use deep Taylor decomposition for text classification tasks.

3.5   INTEGRATED GRADIENTS

The root points in deep Taylor decomposition can be thought of as baselines or reference points. Integrated gradients (Mudrakarta et al., 2018; Sundararajan et al., 2017) also use neutral reference points as baselines: the method simply integrates over the data points connecting our reference to $\mathbf{x_i}$. The data points are weighted by their distance to $\mathbf{x_i}$, putting more weight on data points closest to the data point of interest. Specifically, the integrated gradient along a dimension j for an input $\mathbf{x_i}$ and a neutral reference data point $\mathbf{x_0}$, is

$$(\mathbf{x_i} - \mathbf{x_0}) \times \int_{\alpha=0}^{1} \frac{\delta h(\mathbf{x_0} + \alpha(\mathbf{x_i} - \mathbf{x_0}))}{\delta \mathbf{x}_i^j}.$$

Some authors have proposed improvements to integrated gradients by considering alternative (nonlinear) paths between $\mathbf{x_0}$ and $\mathbf{x_i}$ (Jha et al., 2019).

○ **Open Problem**   Are enhanced integrated gradients derived from alternative paths between $\mathbf{x_0}$ and $\mathbf{x_i}$ beneficial in NLP?

In NLP, integrated gradients have been used widely: it was used to explain the decisions of a large-scale language model in Ramnath et al. (2020); Lu et al. (2020) used integrated gradients to compute influence paths in recurrent architectures; Kobs et al. (2020) used it in the context of paper-venue matching; and so on.

3.6   DEEPLIFT

Deep Taylor decomposition, integrated gradients and DeepLift all consider gradients relative to a neural reference data point or baseline vector x_0. This makes the three approaches different from using vanilla gradients or guided back-propagation, as well as from using layer-wise relevance propagation.[2] DeepLift is therefore also motivated by the observation that a a single weight can be signaling meaningful information even in the regime where its gradient is zero.

Integrated Gradients compute the average partial derivative per feature as on the way from the neutral reference data point to x_i. DeepLIFT, in contrast, approximates this quantity in a single step by replacing the gradient at each nonlinearity with its average value. DeepLIFT can be shown to often be a good approximation of Integrated Gradients (Ancona et al., 2018). DeepLIFT linearizes each node just like deep Taylor decomposition does. Unlike deep Taylor decomposition, however, it does not constrain relevance assigned to each input feature to be positive. Deep Taylor decomposition has several rules to identify root points; DeepLIFT selects root points for linearization such that the sum of the feature relevances equals the difference between the baseline output and the output for x_i.

Poerner et al. (2018) compare this method to other local, gradient-based methods for question answering and morpho-syntactic agreement. They show layer-wise relevance propagation and DeepLift to perform well across these tasks. Kim et al. (2020) use DeepLift, as well as integrated gradients, across two tasks, namely sentiment analysis and inference, and several neural architectures.

---

[2]Extensions of layer-wise relevance propagation, e.g., for neural networks with renormalization layers, rely on decompositions with respect to neural reference data points (Binder et al., 2016).

CHAPTER 4

Global-Backward Explanations

Many global explanation methods rely on the assumption that sparser models are inherently more interpretable. Carvalho et al. (2019) distinguishes between models that are simple enough to be comprehended *holistically*, and models that are more complex, but that can be decomposed into modules that are comprehensible. Obviously, the interpretability of a model—and the value of its explanations—is an empirical question (Jacovi and Goldberg, 2020), but it seems plausible that sparsification *can* be a step toward making a model easier to understand. Previous work has evaluated the interpretability of pruned networks through model visualization, for example.[1] Lage et al. (2019) show a negative correlation between model size and interpretability, but others have questioned whether this correlation holds in general (Freitas, 2013), and it is important to remember that weight pruning strategies are often motivated by other concerns, including making inference faster, and storage and memory requirements smaller (Kim and Hassan, 2020).

Other explainability methods can be used to selects weights that can be pruned. Yeom et al. (2020), for example, use layer-wise relevance propagation (Chapter 3) to select which weights to prune. Similarly, Molchanov et al. (2019) use a method similar to deep Taylor expansion (Chapter 3) to prune networks. Conversely, weight pruning methods and other ways of sparsifying models to make them easier to interpret can also be evaluated by subsequently applying interpretability methods to their representations.

Generally speaking, there are two flavors of pruning methods: *unstructured* pruning methods that prune weights one at a time, disregarding the overall structure of the network, and *structured* pruning methods that prune weights in groups as defined by the neural network architecture. Attention head pruning (Chapter 6) is an example of the latter. While local methods can be used to identify candidate weights to prune, all pruning methods are global, since they change the set of model parameters. In addition, however, pruning methods differ in *when* weights are pruned (before, during or after training), whether multiple iterations of pruning are performed, and whether candidate weights are identified by raw magnitudes (Han et al., 2015), gradients (LeCun et al., 1990), or whether they are somehow learned (Liu et al., 2020).

4.1   POST-HOC UNSTRUCTURED PRUNING

The idea of doing weight pruning based on the magnitude or gradients of the weights after training, has been around since LeCun et al. (1990). I refer to this approach as *post-hoc* unstructured weight pruning. Han et al. (2015) is a good example of this class of methods, relying on raw

[1]https://www.alignmentforum.org/posts/maBNBgopYxb9YZP8B/sparsity-and-interpretability-1

Method	Year	Reference
Sparse coding	1996	Olshausen and Field (1996)
Binary networks	2015	Courbariaux et al. (2015)
Dynamic sparse training	2016	Misra et al. (2016)
Lottery tickets	2019	Frankle and Carbin (2019)

Figure 4.1: Methods: Global Explanations of Training Dynamics.

magnitudes to decide which weights should be pruned. Gordon et al. (2020) and Mao et al. (2020) both use this method to compress language models.

Post-hoc unstructured pruning, of course, does not have to be a one-shot operation. It is perfectly possible to imagine iterating over training and pruning steps, leading to gradually smaller networks. Zhu and Gupta (2017), for example, add a binary weight mask for every layer, which is updated at every training iteration. They simply mask to zero the smallest magnitude weights at that step until some fixed sparsity level is reached.

Obviously, brute-force ablation is also a weight pruning strategy, albeit an expensive one. Several papers have proposed using ablation to identify cells in recurrent architectures that correlate with sentiment or linguistic properties (Kementchedjhieva and Lopez, 2018; Lakretz et al., 2019; Radford et al., 2017). Shibata et al. (2020) extract subspaces of the context vectors c_{t_i} that correlate with linguistic properties.

4.2   LOTTERY TICKETS

The lottery ticket hypothesis (Frankle and Carbin, 2019) refers to the idea that we can sometimes train networks from initialisations that are 10 or 100 times smaller than the full network, with a minimal loss in performance. The method is in its most general form: after training you identify (using some identification method) a subset of weights that you then re-initialize (to their original initial weights, not to *new* random weights); you then retrain the network omitting all other weights. This adds a second perspective to our search through the loss landscape; our search for a decent-sized valley is also a search for a subset of parameters with good initial weights. Encouragingly, Morcos et al. (2019) and others found that these initializations are useful across datasets and tasks. Several identification methods have been proposed for extracting such tickets.

Frankle and Carbin (2019) present an iterative, unstructured pruning method that relies on raw weight magnitudes. The method is simply referred to as *iterative magnitude pruning*. The pruning is done after training, and the magnitudes are the changes in weight magnitudes relative to the random initialization. Frankle et al. (2020) shows that iterative magnitude pruning succeeds in finding good sub-networks if they are stable to noise. In order to make sub-networks more robust, they re-initialize weights to their values at iteration k (for some small k) rather than their values at iteration 0. This is called iterative magnitude pruning with *rewinding*. Rewinding empirically performs well (Renda et al., 2020) and has also seen applications in NLP (Brix et al., 2020). Malach et al. (2020) and Orseau et al. (2020) subsequently showed that for sufficiently large networks, good performance can be achieved *without* training.

Lottery tickets have become very popular in NLP: Yu et al. (2020) successfully applied this weight pruning technique to language modeling and machine translation with recurrent and transformer architectures. Brix et al. (2020) also demonstrated its effectiveness for a transformer architecture used for machine translation. Movva and Zhao (2020) did the same, and showed that the weight pruning lead to more interpretable models. Prasanna et al. (2020) presents lottery ticket experiments for a pre-trained language model.

While lottery ticket-style weight pruning generally leads to sparser models with competitive performance, recent work from outside of NLP suggests the pruned models have a downside: they perform comparatively worse on minority groups. Paganini (2020) evaluates the fairness, i.e., the difference between the best- and worst-case groups, of lottery ticket-style weight pruning for digit recognition problems: specifically, they retrain models for a fixed number of iterations using global unstructured pruning. In addition, they present a meta-regression study suggesting that underrepresented and more complex classes are most severely affected by pruning procedures. See Hooker et al. (2020) for related work and similar results for face recognition.

◯ **Open Problem**   Do lottery tickets increase group disparities in NLP?

Another question is whether lottery tickets have been properly baselined? Evci et al. (2021) suggest that lottery ticket methods simply re-learn the post-hoc pruned network they derive from (§4.1) (and that retraining does not add anything), and argue instead in favor of dynamic sparse training.

4.3   DYNAMIC SPARSE TRAINING

Post-hoc weight pruning induces a network first, then prunes it. The lottery ticket method retrains the network after pruning it, but would it perhaps be superior to jointly train and prune networks? Several papers have in recent years presented variations over the idea that I here refer to as *dynamic sparse training*, i.e., that idea that we can *learn* a binary weight mask during training, not simply by ranking weight magnitudes or performing post-hoc relevance propagation.

Earlier work on dynamic sparse training was mostly about structured pruning: cross-stitch networks (Misra et al., 2016) used special parameters to control sharing between pairs of layers of deep neural networks. The parameters were called *stitches*, stitching together two task-specific neural networks, but can also be thought of as masking sub-networks in a fully shared architecture. Ruder et al. (2018) used a similar approach to make recurrent multi-task learning architectures for NLP tasks better and more sparse, but using smooth indicator functions. These indicator functions were called *sluices* and are directly interpretable. Note that since the indicator functions are smooth, the joint architecture is differentiable in both cases.

Several unstructured pruning methods have been proposed more recently: Auto-Prune (Xiao et al., 2019), for example, learns a binary indicator function that tells you which individual weights can be pruned. A binary (hard) indicator function is not differentiable. The authors use leaky ReLU activation functions to obtain their indicator functions. They show this is superior to using so-called *linear straight-through estimators* (Hubara et al., 2016). Global Sparse Momentum SGD (Ding et al., 2019) is another end-to-end unstructured pruning method. The authors present a novel optimization method, which splits the update rule of momentum SGD into two parts. Momentum SGD adds a coefficient that controls the fraction of gradients retained in every iteration; the authors propose to use the smoothening effects of retraining gradients as an accelerator to boost the passive updates. In each mini-batch, they use a first-order Taylor decomposition to estimate which parameters can be removed with minimal change in loss. This distinguishes active from inactive parameters: active parameters are updated using both the actual gradients and weight decay; passive parameters are only updated with weight decay. This drives inactive parameters toward zero. Azarian et al. (2020) use a relaxation of ℓ_0-regularization to obtain soft masks. Instead of using a step-wise function over the uncompressed weights $\mathbf{w}_{jk}$ after subtracting a pruning threshold τ, they use the sigmoid function with a temperature term T:

$$\mathbf{v}_{jk} = \mathbf{w}_{jk} \cdot \mathrm{sigm}\left(\frac{\mathbf{w}_{jk}^2 - \tau}{T}\right).$$

Bastings et al. (2019), Paranjape et al. (2020), Martins et al. (2020), and Cao et al. (2021) use relaxations of ℓ_0-regularization to induce sparse attention. Ramakrishnan et al. (2020) and Csordás et al. (2021) learn differentiable masks for individual weights and subnetworks, applicable to both structured and unstructured pruning.

In NLP, the structured pruning technique in Ruder et al. (2018) has been used for metaphor identification (Do Dinh and Gurevych, 2016), semantic tagging (Abdou et al., 2018), generating fact checking explanations (Atanasova et al., 2020b), etc. Zhao et al. (2020) use straight-through estimation (Hubara et al., 2016) for domain adaptation and report results on par with fintuning.

○ **Open Problem** Can AutoPrune or Global Sparse Momentum SGD lead to even better performance for language model domain adaptation?

4.4 BINARY NETWORKS AND SPARSE CODING

Binary weights are arguably more interpretable than floats. Courbariaux et al. (2015) and Courbariaux et al. (2016) introduced the idea of learning binarized networks, i.e., with binary weights (and activation functions). While this work (like much work on weight pruning) was mainly motivated by reducing storage requirements and inference time, it is relevant to discuss in the context of global explanations of training dynamics. Binarized networks have been used for language modeling (Liu et al., 2018) and document classification (Shridhar et al., 2020), as well as combined with weight pruning strategies to obtain even smaller and faster models.

Sparse coding is a way of representing x_i by the activation of a small set of neurons. Sparseness is here measured as the average fraction of active neurons. The idea of jointly optimizing for high sparseness and low reconstruction error has been around for a while (Olshausen and Field, 1996), and sparse coding has seen several applications in NLP, e.g., in word and sentence embeddings (Berend, 2017; Murphy et al., 2012; Trifonov et al., 2018). If the sparse coding relies on neurons that correspond to human-interpretable concepts, this of course makes the sparse codes easier to interpret (Apicella et al., 2020).

CHAPTER 5

Local-Forward Explanations of Intermediate Representations

There are bolts and nuts in widely used neural networks that lend themselves easily to interpretation. In this chapter, I focus on methods to visualize or interpret gates and attention in recurrent architectures, as well as attention in transformer architectures. In computer vision, methods have in the same way been developed for convolutions.

5.1   GATES

Quantifying changes in hidden state dynamics is one technique for providing explanations in recurrent networks (Strobelt et al., 2017). Such explanations are at the level of continuous output and are discussed in Chapter 7. In this chapter, I discuss explanations based on *gate activations*. Gates, however, are in some sense not easily interpretable. They add parameters to neural networks, and introduce nonlinear computations that are hard to comprehend holistically. For this reason, researchers have suggested using uptraining methods to interpret gated recurrent networks, e.g., Hou and Zhou (2020). On the other hand, gate activations have been widely used to visualize the inner working of recurrent networks, especially in the context of synthetic (formal) languages (Suzgun et al., 2019; Weiss et al., 2018). Lakretz et al. (2019) visualize gate dynamics to show how language models encode linguistic properties Ghaeini et al. (2018) compare visualizations of input, forget, and output gate activations with attention in natural language inference models. Wang and Jiang (2016) used visualizations of forget gates to arrive at the conclusion that recurrent architectures for natural language inference worked by *remembering important mismatches*, useful for predicting contradictions, while forgetting matching phrases.

5.2   ATTENTION

While there have been several papers that try to use gate values as a vehicle to understand recurrent networks, *attention* (Bahdanau et al., 2015; Vaswani et al., 2017) has attracted the most—well, attention. Even in the seminal paper of Bahdanau et al. (2015), attention was used to shed light on the inner workings of a machine translation architecture. Subsequently, dozens of researchers have used attention weights to analyze the inner workings of recurrent and transformer architectures; see, for example, Rei and Søgaard (2018) for a comparison of gradient-based and attention-based analyses across sentiment analysis and grammatical error correction. While the

Method	Year	Reference
Gates	2016	Wang and Jiang (2016)
Attention	2015	Bahdanau et al. (2015)
Attention roll-out and attention flow	2020	Abnar and Zuidema (2020)
Layer-wise attention tracing	2020	Wu et al. (2020)
Attention decoding	2018	Raganato and Tiedemann (2018)

Figure 5.1: Methods: Global Explanations of Intermediate Representations.

extent to which attention faithfully represents input token importance has been subject of debate (Serrano and Smith, 2019), attention is still widely used to provide explanations (Bastings and Filippova, 2020).

Jain and Wallace (2019) show that attention is often uncorrelated with gradient-based saliency scores, and completely different set of attention weights often result in the same predictions. This was also shown in Serrano and Smith (2019), and Moradi et al. (2019) showed similar results for machine translation. Pruthi et al. (2020a) explicitly showed how to manipulate attention weights to provide deceitful explanations without hurting performance.

Vashishth et al. (2019) makes the interesting point that attention seems to be less important (and therefore less effective in providing explanations) for sequence classification tasks, than for bi-sequence classification or sequence-to-sequence problems. Other researchers have proposed ways to make attention more amenable for explanation. Kobayashi et al. (2020), for example, remind us that attention is a weighted sum of transformed vectors, and that the attention weights interact with the vector norms to produce attention. Taking this into account, attention aligns better with salience, it seems. Mohankumar et al. (2020) modify the LSTM objective to explicitly diversify hidden representations across time steps and show through heuristic evaluations how this makes attention more predictive of input token importance. Brunner et al. (2020) show that attention can be decomposed into a component that is independent of the output, and propose to rely only on the remainder, which they call *effective attention*, for deriving explanations. Attention flow (Abnar and Zuidema, 2020), which I explain next, is another attempt to make attention more predictive of input token importance.

5.3   ATTENTION ROLL-OUT AND ATTENTION FLOW

In multi-layer transformer architectures, information about input tokens is quickly mixed, and attention weights at different layers can therefore be unreliable if not interpreted properly. Attention flow and layer-wise attention training (§5.4) are methods for computing more reliable attention weights. Abnar and Zuidema (2020) propose two different algorithms for this: attention roll-out and attention flow.

In attention roll-out, Abnar and Zuidema (2020) compute the attention associated with a particular position, i.e., a particular time step t at some layer l by an attention head h, $\mathbf{A}^l_{h(t)}$, by summing over all multiplications of edge weights along a path connecting the current position with higher (connected) positions in the network. In attention flow, in contrast, maximum flow values are used to represent attention. This means that to compute $\mathbf{A}^l_{h(t)}$, we rely on the maximum path, i.e., the largest multiplication of edge weights, rather than the sum of all possible path weights.

Both methods lead to less mixed attention weights at higher layers, i.e., more distinct attention patterns. The authors show that roll-out and maximum flow values correlate much better than raw attention weights—with both gradient-based methods and the effect of leaving out input tokens on output. Attention roll-out is faster than attention flow, and the evaluations in Abnar and Zuidema (2020) suggest that there is little reason to choose attention flow over attention roll-out. DeRose et al. (2020) present a similar method for backward computation of attention flow, as well as per-instance visualizations thereof.

5.4   LAYER-WISE ATTENTION TRACING

Remember (from §2.1.3 in Chapter 2) how a self-attention layer in a transformer architecture consists of three sets (matrices) of model parameters, $\mathbf{w}^q$ (for query vectors), $\mathbf{w}^k$ (for key vetors), and $\mathbf{w}^v$ (for value vectors). This gives us three vector representations of each time step or input token. We then calculate the attention distributed from the time step t in our input example $\mathbf{x}_i$ by taking the dot product of t's query vector and the key vector of all other time steps, and normalizing these values to produce an attention distribution α. We then multiply in the value vectors and pass the resulting vector on to the next layer.

When computing layer-wise attention we move backward. Our transformer architecture turns an input sequence $\mathbf{x}_i$ into a representation. The attention that contributed to this representation can be divided back to each attention head h at position t according to the value of α in this position, i.e., the attention distribution at t. The attention coming from higher layers at head h, position t, layer l, say $\mathbf{A}^l_{h(t)}$ is the weighted sum of all $\mathbf{A}^{l+1}_{h(t')}$, where the weight is given by $\alpha_{h(t \to t')}$. This procedure distributes attention all the way back to the input tokens.

Since computing the sum of the attention path scores is equivalent to tracking a layer-wise redistribution of the attention weights, this approach is equivalent to doing attention roll-out (Abnar and Zuidema, 2020).

○ **Observation**   Layer-wise attention training and attention roll-out (§6.1) are the same method.

5.5   ATTENTION DECODING

In order to see to what extent certain attention heads encode for syntactic information, Raganato and Tiedemann (2018) suggested using maximum spanning tree algorithms–originally proposed for syntactic dependency parsing in McDonald et al. (2005)—to decode the best hierarchical structures induced from the $n \times n$ dense graphs by single attention heads for sentences with n words. Htut et al. (2019) followed up on this work, experimenting with more language models. Ravishankar et al. (2021) decode attention flow scores (Abnar and Zuidema, 2020) instead of attention weights and extend their analysis to multilingual language models before and after fine-tuning with dependency parsing objectives. They show that grammatical relations are often encoded or reflected by the same attention heads across languages, and fine-tuning makes it easier to decode this information.

CHAPTER 6

Global-Forward Explanations of Intermediate Representations

In Chapter 5, gate activations and attention weights were referred to as *intermediate representations*. Global explanations at the level of such intermediate representations tend to address which gates and attention heads are discriminative, and which are redundant and dispensable: examples would include sentences such as *These gates are used to implement counting* or *This model relies heavily on a single attention head*. The extent to which gates or attention heads can be removed, tells us a lot about the inner workings of a neural network.

The removal of gates or attention heads is commonly referred to as *pruning*. Some of the heuristic evaluation strategies discussed in Chapter 11 involve the *removal* of input tokens. The idea is simply that explanation methods that attribute relevance to input tokens, can be evaluated in part by whether removing the input tokens predicted to be relevant, has more of an effect on the output, than removing input tokens predicted not to be relevant. I argue the pruning strategies discussed in this chapter can be thought of in two ways: as (a) methods for obtaining simpler models that are more likely to be comprehended holistically, and as (b) ways to evaluate local explainability methods, typically those based on training dynamics.

6.1 GATE PRUNING

While there is a growing literature on attention head pruning, there is not really literature on gate pruning. Previous work on pruning recurrent neural models, at least in NLP, has not singled out gates, but rather evaluated general weight pruning strategies (Chapter 4). See et al. (2016), for example, use relatively simple magnitude-based weight pruning schemes in the context of neural machine translation based on LSTM architectures, but they analyze the pruning rates of different types of parameters, and show that gates are particularly important at the outermost layers of their networks. Zhang and Stadie (2019) also study general GRU weight pruning and observe that various normalization techniques are crucial to prevent too aggressive pruning of GRU gates, in particular for the update gates $\mathbf{w}^z$. These techniques lead to sparse connections being more evenly distributed across the weight matrix.

Method	Year	Reference
Gate pruning	2016	See et al. (2016)
Attention head pruning	2019	Voita et al. (2019)

Figure 6.1: **Methods: Global Explanations of Intermediate Representations.**

○ **Open Problem**   Would gate pruning, e.g., using dynamic sparse training techniques such as Voita et al. (2019), lead to more interpretable recurrent architectures?

6.2   ATTENTION HEAD PRUNING

In Chapter 4, I covered standard weight pruning algorithms. Here I instead focus on the pruning and analysis of the *intermediate* representations that are special to the neural networks employed in NLP. In fact, while there has been some work on pruning gates, e.g., Dai et al. (2018) and Riera et al. (2019), I focus on attention here.

Voita et al. (2019) use layer-wise relevance propagation to identify the least relevant attention heads for subsequent pruning.

Michel et al. (2019) show that we can use simple gradients (Chapter 3) to effectively prune attention heads; Hao et al. (2021) use integrated gradients (Chapter 3) for this. These are two-stage methods, using accumulated statistics from running local methods over samples of data to perform global pruning. Gordon et al. (2020) study the effect of general magnitude-based processing of language models (Chapter 4) before and after fine-tuning, but their analysis focuses on the effect of head pruning.

Voita et al. (2019) rely on layer-wise relevance propagation (Chapter 3) to identify less relevant attention heads (but do not use this method to prune the heads). As pointed out in Voita et al. (2019), the local methods used for attention head analysis and pruning are not applied to identify important input regions, but to compute the relevance of neurons or model components. In fact, Voita et al. (2019) do not propagate relevance scores all the way back to the input variables, but stop at the layer of interest. Voita et al. (2019) analyze attention heads trained for machine translation and identify heads with different roles, such as encoding positions, grammatical relations, or attributing attention to rare tokens. As mentioned, they do not, however, use the propagated relevance scores to directly prune the heads. Instead they use regularized gates in a way similar to dynamic sparse training (Chapter 4) to learn Transformer models that rely on fewer attention heads. Treviso and Martins (2020) use a sparsity-inducing regularizer to learn a *recurrent* model with a more interpretable (because sparse) attention function.

Budhraja et al. (2020), however, question how direct the relation between the importance of attention heads and their prunability. They show that a large fraction of the attention heads can be randomly pruned with limited effect on accuracy, and that there is little difference between pruning random heads and more relevant heads. There is a fundamental difference between the experiments reported in Budhraja et al. (2020) and the experiments reported in Michel et al. (2019) and Hao et al. (2021): Budhraja et al. (2020) evaluate models that are fine-tuned *after* attention head pruning; Michel et al. (2019) and Hao et al. (2021) do not. This suggests that gradient-based methods can identify less relevant attention heads that can be pruned without affecting performance much, and that fine-tuning can also, perhaps unsurprisingly, compensate for removing relevant attention heads.

CHAPTER 7

Local-Forward Explanations of Continuous Output

As already discussed, neural networks are also representation learners. Transformers, for example, can be used for classification, sequence labeling, or generation, but they also produce text encodings, i.e., continuous output vectors, which can be used directly for a range of tasks, e.g., synonymy detection, word alignment, bilingual dictionary induction, sentence retrieval, document retrieval. This chapter presents several (very different) techniques for interpreting neural networks at the level of input encodings or continuous output vectors.

7.1 WORD ASSOCIATION NORMS

The performance improvements from using word embeddings (Turian et al., 2010) helped spark the NLP community's interest in representation learning. Word embeddings, as a branch of distributional semantics (Evert, 2010), represent words in a vector space such that related words are close. NLP models that take word embeddings as input, can learn to generalize across regions of this vector space. Word association norms, i.e., psycho-linguistic studies of human word-to-word associations, is a standard way to evaluate distributional semantics, an idea first proposed in Church and Hanks (1989). Given human associations or human similarity or relatedness scores, we can either compute how association strengths correlate between humans and models, or how human associations are ranked by the word embedding models. Whether it is better to think of correlations with word association norms as an extrinsic *evaluation* of language models or an *analysis* or interpretation thereof, is not entirely clear to me, but such correlations have often been used to explain or characterize the weaknesses of language models. Hartmann and Søgaard (2018), for instance, use this technique to show that visually grounded language models are much better at representing concrete nouns than any other parts of speech.

7.2 WORD ANALOGIES

A word analogy is a quadruple of words, e.g., *Berlin*, *Germany*, *Paris*, and *France*, that stand in a pair-wise analogous relationship. Berlin is the capital of Germany, for example; analogously, Paris is the capital of France. This analogy works in both directions, e.g., Germany is the country governed by the government in Berlin, just like France is the country governed by the govern-

Method	Year	Reference
Word association norms	1987	Church and Hanks (1989)
Word analogies	2013	Mikolov et al. (2013a)
Time step dynamics	2017	Strobelt et al. (2017)

Figure 7.1: Methods: Local Explanations of Continuous Outputs. Direct evaluations of continuous outputs, no representative sample is required (but may be leveraged for corpus-level statistics).

ment in Paris. Others work only in one direction. The above analogy is semantic, but researchers have also explored morphosyntactic analogies, e.g., *run* is to *ran*, what *swim* is to *swam*.

We can query language models to see if they reflect the semantic or morphosyntactic relations encoded by word analogies in the following way: if we take the vector representations of *Berlin*, *Germany*, *Paris*, and *France*, and assume the analogous relationships are encoded the same way, then the difference between the vectors for the two pairs of countries and capitals should be the same way. In other words, we can query whether we obtain the vector for *France* by subtracting the vector for *Germany* from the vector for *Berlin* and then adding the vector for *Paris*, or vice versa. While it is unlikely this produces exactly the vector for *France*, we can ask, alternatively, whether the vector for *France* is the nearest neighbor to this offset vector.

Like word association norms, word analogies can perhaps be argued to be an evaluation of language models, but they are often used to analyze language models (Mikolov et al., 2013a). Using the above vector offset method, researchers have analyzed to what extent language models encode various semantic or morphosyntactic relations (Drozd et al., 2016), for example, show that three common word embedding models encode the capital-of relation in the above example very consistently, as well as morphosyntactic relations that pertain to inflectional morphology; for other semantic and morphosyntactic relations, the encoding is much less consistent.

While many initial analyses using word analogies were flawed (Rogers et al., 2017), word analogy datasets have been refined in recent work (Fournier et al., 2020; Garneau et al., 2021), e.g., zooming in on bidirectional analogies. Analogies have also been proposed to evaluate sentence encodings (Zhu and de Melo, 2020).

7.3   TIME STEP DYNAMICS

Several researchers have proposed methods for quantifying *time step dynamics* in recurrent neural networks. By this they mean to refer to significant changes in activation across the time steps of a specific input sequence. The simplest possible method for this, for example, is simply plotting the activations (Strobelt et al., 2017), but more sophisticated methods have been proposed more recently.

Murdoch et al. (2018) partition the activation value of each output or hidden state in a part that is caused by some selected token or phrase in focus, and a part that is not. The technique, which is called *contextual decomposition*, is based on a linearization of the activation functions that enables this partitioning. It is computationally expensive, though, since a forward pass has to be run once for every time step. Kádár et al. (2017) rely on word omission scores to quantify time step dynamics. Saphra and Lopez (2020) propose a decompositional interdependence measure to quantify dependencies between time steps in recurrent networks. The measure is defined over hidden state representations.

CHAPTER 8

Global-Forward Explanations of Continuous Output

Neural networks produce vectors or representations. On a sample of input examples, they produce distributions of vectors. Such point clouds of vectors can also be interpreted. If we consider *two* such clouds, we can quantify the extent to which they are structurally similar, for example. Or we can learn clusters of vectors and analyze the clusters manually, or use these to compute functions that enable us to extract influential data points for our test examples.

8.1 CORRELATION OF REPRESENTATIONS

We can learn about properties of our models by correlation point clouds across vocabularies or samples with baseline point clouds, e.g., external reference points. This holds not only for word embedding models, but for any neural network with one or more hidden layers that map individual words or sentences to vectors. For example, we can ask if humans represent words or sentences in ways similar to how humans organize them by correlating point clouds with fMRI signals (Abnar et al., 2019; Gauthier and Levy, 2019; Hollenstein et al., 2019; Søgaard, 2016) (glossing over the non-trivial relation between fMRI and how humans organize information), we can correlate representations across models or layers (Abdou et al., 2019), or we can see how similar point clouds are across languages (Vulić et al., 2020).

One simple method for quantifying the similarity of point clouds is to see whether we can learn a linear regression from one to the other (Søgaard, 2016). This amounts to learning a linear transformation from one vector space into the other in a way similar to how linear projections are learned for cross-lingual embeddings (Mikolov et al., 2013a). See Søgaard et al. (2019) for a book-length discussion of linear projections and related methods, including both supervised and unsupervised ones. Other methods introduce fewer parameters and more directly measure the extent to which two point clouds are structurally similar.

Abnar et al. (2019) and Abdou et al. (2019), for example, both use a method for correlating vector distributions called *representational similarity analysis*, originally proposed in Kriegeskorte et al. (2008): this method computes the (nonparametric) correlation coefficient across the pairwise distances in the aligned point clouds. Intuitively, if two sentences are represented similarly in your neural network, this method can be used to quantify the extent to which, in general, these two sentences are also similar in other vector space, e.g., a dataset of fMRI recordings.

Method	Year	Reference
Correlation of representations	2013	Mikolov et al. (2013a)
Clustering	2017	Trost and Klakow (2017)
Probing classifiers	2017	Belinkov et al. (2017)
Concept activation	2018	Kim et al. (2018)
Influential examples	2018	Yeh et al. (2018)

Figure 8.1: Methods: Global Explanations of Continuous Outputs. All methods induce parameters—from correlation coefficients to complex task-specific models—based on continuous representations from the underlying model.

8.2   CLUSTERING

Several of the concept activation approaches discussed below rely on clustering as an integral step in deriving explanations, but there is also considerable work on simply clustering the continuous output of NLP models: Trost and Klakow (2017), for example, use clostering to analyze word embeddings. Aharoni and Goldberg (2020), for example, use clustering to see how large-scale language models encode textual domains. Yenicelik et al. (2020) use clustering to see how large-scale language models encode for semantics. Hiebert et al. (2018) cluster time steps by output gate activations to analyze how recurrent networks generalize.

8.3   PROBING CLASSIFIERS

Probing classifiers (Ettinger et al., 2016) learn to *classify* continuous output vectors from supervision—rather than how to cluster them in the absence of supervision. The core intuition behind probing is if we can learn simple (typically linear) classifiers that predict properties with high accuracy (say, > 0.9) from the representations of a neural network, then this neural network has, in a sense, learned this property. In recent years there has been a lot of studies using probing classifiers to see whether language models encode various properties, both in NLP and related fields, such as computer vision (Alain and Bengio, 2017). Belinkov et al. (2017), for example, evaluated to what extent morphosyntactic and semantic information was reflected in machine translation models. Tenney et al. (2019) is perhaps an even better example of this line of work, using linear classifiers to show how a particular large-scale language model provides very useful representations for a wide range of NLP tasks. Jawahar et al. (2019) present a very similar study, and Ravishankar et al. (2019) extend such studies to multiple languages.

The extent to which the success of probing classifiers, say in discriminating between sentences with and without relative clauses, says something about the extent to which *they encode for* relative clauses, has been discussed. Kunz and Kuhlmann (2020), for example, suggest that the success of probing classifiers trained on large-scale language models is likely a side-effect of their capacity for representing and memorizing contexts.

Belinkov (2021) discuss probing classifiers and their limitations at length, including the importance of properly baselining probing classifiers to put their performance into perspective. If probing classifiers achieve good performance on random representations, the fact that they also achieve good performance on the representations from your neural network, does not tell you much about what your neural network has learned. See Hewitt and Liang (2019) for work on baselining the performance of probing classifiers. It remains an open problem, however, how to best probe for linguistic properties (Elazar et al., 2021; Pimentel et al., 2020).

○ **Open Problem**   What is the most reliable method for probing for linguistic properties?

8.4   CONCEPT ACTIVATION

The idea behind concept activation is to generalize across examples by pointing to abstract concepts that describe these examples. As such, it is related to clustering, except that the methods described here require supervision and are based on deriving a loss from discrete output predictions of auxiliary classifiers. Since these are auxiliary classifiers relying on the representations (continuous output) of our models, we classify these as global explanations of continuous output. Concept activation are even more similar to the probing classifiers we just discussed. In fact, you can think of concept activation as training a set of linear of probing classifiers to distinguish concepts, and a way to attribute relevance to a set of concepts based on these classifiers.

Kim et al. (2018) present an approach to interpreting continuous model output based on so-called *concept activation vectors*. Concept activation vectors are simply vectors in the direction of the examples associated with particular concepts. They are obtained by training a linear classifier between the examples associated with a concept and random counter examples and then taking the vector that is orthogonal to the decision boundary of the linear classifier. The probability of a class given a vector (the directionality of the derivative of the logit layer) now intuitively means how would the probability of the class would change if I make the picture a little more like the concept or a little like the concept. While this idea makes intuitive sense in continuous input spaces, it is perhaps a little less intuitive in the context of text, where the concept activation vectors would enable us to ask questions such as whether the probability of positive sentiment by making a review more or less technical, for example.

Goyal et al. (2020) build directly on Kim et al. (2018), but argue their original proposal was prone to confounding, i.e., unfaithful (see Chapter 12 for a discussion of faithfulness). In response, they present a causal effect model that approximately learns the effect of the presence or absence of concepts by using a variational autoencoder. Auto-encoders have been used in the context of both local and global methods to make them less sensitive to confounding. See Alvarez-Melis and Jaakkola (2017) and Shankaranarayana and Runje (2019) for a similar extensions of LIME, for example. See Moraffah et al. (2020) for an overview of this line of work.

Ghorbani et al. (2019) present an approach to concept activation for computer vision that, while similar to Kim et al. (2018), does not require any supervision. Instead of supervision, they rely on multi-level segmentation of the input images. They then cluster the segments and return these as concept vectors in the same way as was done in Kim et al. (2018).

Koh et al. (2020) present a more radical model in which the predicted concepts are used to make the final class prediction. In their architecture, a concept distribution is first predicted, which is fed into a linear classifier mapping these distributions onto the output space.

While concept activation methods are technically very similar to probing classifiers, they have not seen widespread adoption in the NLP community. In part, this may be because many concepts of relevance to NLP tasks are hard to think of in a continuous way; for example, what would it mean to be more or less a relative clause? Schwarzenberg et al. (2019b), though, present a method for probing language models based on concept activations, and Bashier et al. (2020) uses unsupervised concept activation vectors in the context of document classification. I leave it as an open problem what other applications of concept activations there might be in NLP.

○ **Open Problem**   What are meaningful applications of concept activations in NLP?

8.5   INFLUENTIAL EXAMPLES

Chapter 9 discusses methods for generating influential training data points for test examples, providing explanations for model decisions in terms of training instances. Popular methods include *influence sketching* (Wojnowicz et al., 2016) and *influence functions* (Koh and Liang, 2017). These local methods are very slow, however. Yeh et al. (2018) presents a faster alternative to detecting influential examples, compared to influence sketching and influence functions. They train neural networks with ℓ_2 regularization and show how this guarantees the output can be approximated well by a linear decomposition into training data point activations. Their method is global, since the decomposition is learned once and for all.

Pruthi et al. (2020b) present another global method for computing influential examples. Instead of a linear decomposition, they rely on training checkpoints and a held-out data set that enables them to correlate training examples with loss changes on unseen examples. Unlike the method in Yeh et al. (2018), their method is not fully *post-hoc*, since it relies on extracting checkpoints of the training procedure. Both approaches rely on the outermost softmax layers of the explained models.

The relation between global methods for finding influential examples and concept activation methods has to the best of my knowledge not previously been discussed, but it seems to me the two subclasses are non-trivially, yet intimately, related: explaining with influential examples and explaining with concepts seem to form two points on a continuum: the approach to concept activation in Ghorbani et al. (2019), for example, uses clusters of segments (found in the training data) as concepts and learn concept activation vectors by training a linear classifier for each cluster. If in Yeh et al. (2018), we think of each training example as a cluster or concept activation vector, how then do these two approaches relate?

○ **Open Problem**   What is the exact relationship between methods for generating concept activation vectors and methods for generating influential examples?

CHAPTER 9

Local-Forward Explanations of Discrete Output

Say you realize your language model behaves oddly in the context of a sentence that begins with the character +. You may hypothesize that the language model is generally sensitive to mathematical symbols appearing in first positions in input sentences. To test this, what would you do? One obvious thing to do is to sample n sentences and design a test data set of $(k + 1) \times n$ input examples, k examples for each of the original sentences. The number k would refer to a set of predefined mathematical symbols. If the sentence *John loves Mary* was sampled, the test data set would also include + *John loves Mary*, × *John loves Mary*, etc. The model's performance on this data set and its k subsets would enable you to determine if your hypothesis is plausible or implausible. What you have produced, is sometimes called a *challenge dataset* in the NLP literature, and it illustrates how we can explain model decisions based on the model's *discrete output* across a set of local (non-representative) input examples.

9.1   CHALLENGE DATASETS

Challenge datasets are collections of particularly hard or interesting examples, designed to test models for their ability to cope with specific phenomena. The phenomena of interest obviously differ across NLP tasks.

In the context of language models, Goldberg (2019), for example, examines the ability of a particular language model to capture subject-verb agreement phenomena in English. van Schijndel et al. (2019) discuss the performance of a range of language models across a suite of different linguistic constructions in English. Warstadt et al. (2019), in contrast, design fill-in-the-gap examples for the phenomenon of negative polarity item licensing and evaluate language models across carefully designed examples highlighting various aspects of this phenomenon, also. Chaves (2020) uses surprisal studies to see whether English language models based on recurrent architectures learn about filler-gap constructions. The challenge datasets designed for language models are sometimes referred to as *fill-in-the-gap probes* (Rogers et al., 2020). See Hu et al. (2020) for a nice survey of existing challenge datasets for English language modeling and a benchmarking of commonly used language models.

For question answering and natural language inference, for example, challenge datasets have focused on examples that violate specific heuristics that models are likely to learn (McCoy

Method	Year	Reference
Challenge datasets	2018	Naik et al. (2018)
Local uptraining	2016	Ribeiro et al. (2016)
Influential examples	2017	Koh and Liang (2017)

Figure 9.1: Methods: Local Explanations of Discrete Outputs. These methods directly interpret discrete output on particular datasets. Some methods (e.g., LIME) induce additional parameters, but from perturbations rather than representative samples.

et al., 2019), numerical reasoning (Dua et al., 2019; Naik et al., 2018), or negation (Gururangan et al., 2018; Naik et al., 2018).

While most challenge datasets are typically designed to evaluate task-specific NLP models across a few or maybe a dozen challenging phenomena, González et al. (2020) instead presents a *multi-task* (and multi-lingual) challenge dataset focusing instead on a single linguistic phenomenon, namely reflexive pronouns. Ribeiro et al. (2020) present a comprehensive guide for constructing challenge datasets for NLP tasks.

9.2   LOCAL UPTRAINING

In the next chapter (§10.1), I discuss a strategy for learning simple approximations of neural networks called *uptraining* (Petrov et al., 2010). Uptraining refers to the idea of training a simple model on the output of the more complex model h to obtain enough supervision to learn a good approximation of h. In this section, I discuss a very influential *local* explanation method called LIME (Ribeiro et al., 2016) and its offspring. As I will show, these methods perform *uptraining on perturbations of a single example*. This approximates the decision boundary locally, but is different from standard uptraining in that it does not rely on *i.i.d.* samples. In Chapter 12, I argue that these methods, along with all other local methods, cannot, strictly speaking, be unfaithful. The random sampling of perturbations in these methods is really just a hack to approximate the analytical solution.

The Local Model-agnostic Explanations (LIME) method (Ribeiro et al., 2016) has become one of the most widely used post-hoc model interpretability methods in NLP. LIME aims to interpret model predictions by locally approximating a model's decision boundary around an individual prediction. This is done by training a linear classifier on perturbations of this example. Since the units of attribution in text are words, the perturbations are obtained by randomly removing words. When training the linear classifier, say a logistic regression model, the examples are weighted by the inverse of their distance to the original input example.

Several weaknesses of LIME have been identified in the literature: LIME is linear (Bramhall et al., 2020), unstable (Elshawi et al., 2019), and very sensitive to the width of the kernel used to assign weights to input example perturbations (Kopper, 2019; Vlassopou-los, 2019), an increasing number of features also increases weight instability (Gruber, 2019), and Vlassopoulos (2019) argues that with sparse data, sampling is insufficient. Laugel et al. (2018) argues the specific sampling technique is suboptimal. Moreover, LIME is computation-ally expensive. Nevertheless, LIME has remained extremely popular (Dieber and Kirrane, 2020).

Poerner et al. (2018), in addition to comparing gradient-based methods, introduce an extension of LIME for recurrent architectures, based on sampling substrings rather than words. Bramhall et al. (2020) extend LIME by fitting quadractic functions rather than linear functions to the local decision boundary. Alvarez-Melis and Jaakkola (2017) and Shankaranarayana and Runje (2019) have present causal extensions of LIME relying on variational autoencoders.

9.3   INFLUENTIAL EXAMPLES

Explanations do not have to be in the form of input token importance attributions (or, more generally, in the form of extractive or abstractive rationales; see Chapter 11), or of model visual-izations. If you ask me why I think a sentence s is ungrammatical, I can either point to the words that I think make it ungrammatical (in context), or I can point to the examples that taught me examples such as s are ungrammatical. Methods for finding such influential examples are mostly local explanations of discrete output. That is, they find the examples that were influential for an individual model decision, and they do so by correlating training examples with discrete output.

The simplest way to see the influence of a training example is to train without it. This form of *leave-one-out* training is conceptually simple and simple to implement, but unfortunately, it is extremely expensive for large training data sets. The effect of deleting a training example x_i is sometimes referred to as *Cook's distance*; this is calculated as the sum of all changes (over a population or a sample thereof) induced by removing x_i.

Wojnowicz et al. (2016) came up with an approximation of Cook's distance that worked for large-scale regression datasets, by injecting random projections. Koh and Liang (2017) pro-pose a few tricks to efficiently compute influence functions, a technique from robust statistics for estimating how model parameter are affected by upweighting a training point. Exact compu-tation of influence functions relies on computing the inverse Hessian matrix, which is expensive, but Koh and Liang (2017) instead propose to compute Hessian vector products instead of ex-plicitly computing the entire matrix. Guo et al. (2020) and Han et al. (2020) present additional hacks for faster computation of influence function, as well as application to large-scale language models. Basu et al. (2020) introduce a way of computing second order influence functions for detecting influential subsets of examples.

Influence sketching and influence functions are both local explanation method in that they compute explanations for individual data points. This makes them slow. Global methods for detecting influential examples (for test data points) have been proposed, though, and I covered some of these in Chapter 8.

CHAPTER 10

Global-Forward Explanations of Discrete Output

Other approaches to explaining the decisions of h are motivated by the simple idea of learning an approximation of h' that is so simple that it can be comprehended holistically. Obviously, the faithfulness of h' depends on the extent to which it agrees with h, e.g., its loss relative to h, $\ell(h(\mathbf{x}_i), h'(\mathbf{x}_i))$. Some approaches explicitly minimize this loss through a process, sometimes referred to as *uptraining* of h' (Petrov et al., 2010). Related work trains a model h' to predict the performance of h based on data set characteristics. The approximation h' does not provide local explanations in this case, but a high-level error analysis of h known as a *meta-analysis*.

10.1 UPTRAINING

The core idea behind the post-hoc interpretability technique of uptraining is simple: apply your final hypothesis h to (a large set of) unlabeled data U, and fit a model h' from a simpler ("inherently interpretable") hypothesis class to the predictions of h. Since U can be much larger than the original training data D, this increases the chance that we can find a reasonable approximation of h within our simpler hypothesis class. If the hypothesis class is sufficiently simple, it may be possible to holistically comprehend h', e.g., by model visualization.

Ba and Caruana (2014) use this technique to learn shallow neural networks from deeper ones. Frosst and Hinton (2017) learn a decision tree from the predictions of a neural network on unlabeled data. In NLP, the idea goes at least back to Petrov et al. (2010). In more recent literature, uptraining has become extremely popular under the banner of *knowledge distillation*: Kim and Rush (2016), for example, uptrains word-level and sequence-level models for machine translation and combine this with weight pruning. Tang et al. (2019) uptrains a simple recurrent language model by training on examples sampled from much larger transformer-based language models. Wu et al. (2020), also the context of machine translation, explore doing uptraining with supervision from multiple layers of the original model.

Others have explored *jointly* training the simple and the complex models. Li et al. (2020), for example, present a method where knowledge is alternately transferred between decision trees and neural networks. A similar idea was explored in Wang et al. (2018). Lan et al. (2018) takes things one step further, learning a multi-branch network of simple models and using the ensemble as a teacher, but note how this is no longer an explanation method, since there is no complex

Method	Year	Reference
Uptraining	2010	Petrov et al. (2010)
Meta-analysis	2012	Kolachina et al. (2012)
Downstream evaluation	2020	Fu et al. (2020)

Figure 10.1: Methods: Global Explanations of Discrete Outputs. Multi-task or multi-domain datasets can be used to say something about how well a model generalizes; meta-analysis goes beyond this and analyzes *what* in a dataset is predictive of model error.

model knowledge distillation is used to simplify. Conversely, the ensembles are *created* from the simpler models.

10.2   META-ANALYSIS

The idea of meta-analysis is to induce a regressor to predict the performance of our model on different batches or data sets. The data sets are typically featurized along relevant data set characteristics, but this can also include the occurrence of concepts or overlaps with clusters (Chapter 8), for example. It is common to use simple linear regression, but ℓ_1-regularized regression (lasso regression) or group lasso regression lead to sparser and more interpretable explanations.

Meta-analysis has been used to analyze a wide range of neural NLP architectures and models, including machine translation architectures and their sensitivity to the amount of training data available (Kolachina et al., 2012); multi-task recurrent networks and their sensitivity to the characteristics of the task-specific data (Bingel and Søgaard, 2017); cross-lingual zero-shot applications of models and their sensitivity to cross-lingual differences (Lauscher et al., 2020); etc.

10.3   DOWNSTREAM EVALUATION

Papers on explainable NLP are often motivated by a need to go beyond mere performance figures, say an F_1 score on a common benchmark. We not only want to know how good models are, but what they are good at, where they fail, and how they can be improved. However, while a single performance figure is not particularly informative, a large set of such numbers may be. In the limit, all practically different models can be distinguished by their performance across data sets, and performance figures across a decent-sized collection of data sets often tell us which models are likely to have picked up on some of the same things (Zhou et al., 2020). We can also compare the outputs of models to each other, giving us even more information about how models relate (Fu et al., 2020). Using multiple benchmarks also provide much better grounds for testing whether a model is significantly better than another (Søgaard et al., 2014).

CHAPTER 11

Evaluating Explanations

Model performance metrics are functions from pairs of instances of data structures to real numbers, typically in [0,1]. These functions thus abstract away from the models themselves. The same holds for the metrics we use to evaluate explanations. The metrics are, in other words, orthogonal to the taxonomy presented here. In this chapter, we therefore introduce a classification of explanations (not methods), distinguishing, for example, explanations in terms of input subsegments (so-called *extractive rationales*), e.g., from LIME, and explanations in terms of training instances, e.g., from influence functions. Since the explanation classes are somewhat informal (compared to taxonomy presented here), I simply refer to them as *flavors*.

We subsequently discuss the different evaluation methodologies that have been proposed. I follow Doshi-Velez and Kim (2017) in making a three-way distinction: while they talk about functionally grounded, human-grounded, and application-grounded evaluations, I will discuss using heuristics, human annotations, and human experiments. Functionally, grounded evaluations correspond well to the notion of heuristic evaluations, discussed here, but while using human annotations count as *human-grounded* in Doshi-Velez and Kim (2017), so do some of our human experiments. The category of human experiments is, in other words, a union of a subset of human-grounded evaluations and (all of) application grounded evaluations. Since linguistic annotations occupy a special role in NLP, traditionally, I believe this three-way divide is more useful in our context than the one proposed in Doshi-Velez and Kim (2017).

11.1 FLAVORS OF EXPLANATIONS

First, however, it is important to consider the syntax of explanations. In computer vision, explanations often take the form of saliency maps. Similarly, explanations in NLP are often in the form of a mark-up of the input example highlighting important regions (text spans) or words. I follow DeYoung et al. (2020) and call such explanations *extractive rationales* and distinguish them from three other types of explanations: abstractive rationales, training instances, and model visualizations.[1]

---

[1]Jacovi and Goldberg (2021) criticize the use of the term *rationale* and instead propose *highlighting*, which they find less misleading. I fully agree that the term *rationale* is suggestive, but so is most words used in this book. Consider the title: *Explainable Natural Language Processing*. The word *explainable* is used by English language users in a variety of contexts, referring to very different levels of knowledge; the word *natural* is, when you think about it, odd in the context of a book that is mostly written language; even the word *language* is a bit of stretch in the context of disembodied, finite samples of sentences or paragraphs, taken from narrow textual domains; and what is meant by *processing* is certainly different from what is meant by the same term in the psychological literature.

Extractive Rationales   Extractive rationales are similar to saliency maps in computer vision. They highlight regions in our input examples x_i that are deemed particular relevant for the prediction. Such rationales are produced, for example, when passing vanilla gradients or attention weights back to the input layer (Rei and Søgaard, 2018).

Formally, extractive rationales can either be a subset or substring of the input, or it can be an assignment of weights (relevance attribution scores) to words or phrases. The output of LIME, for example, is a word-level relevance scoring. In human evaluations, it is common, however, to only highlight the top-k (3, 5, maybe 10) most relevant words; these words are then either marked in the same way, reflecting equal importance, or in a graded way, e.g., using heatmap-like coloring, to reflect estimated degrees of importance (Lai and Tan, 2019). Providing human with sparse rationales, by limiting the highlighting to the top-k most relevant words, is often motivated by the assumption that rationales need to be simple to be comprehensible (Lei et al., 2016).

Murdoch et al. (2018) discuss evaluation of recurrent models and go beyond just using words as rationales, arguing that previous attribution methods treat recurrent models as if they were bag-of-words models, and ignore the exact thing they are designed to capture, namely compositionality. They instead assign importance scores to phrases by contextual decomposition (Chapter 7). Similarly, Chen et al. (2020) also go beyond just presenting highlighted words, and represent extractive rationales in the form of highlighted tree structures to visualize the effects of composition. From a linguistic perspective, there is a clear relationship between such explanations, based on syntax, and explanations based on semantic concepts. Since the units of surface syntax correspond to substrings of our input examples, I think of the above explanations as extractive rationales, whereas explanations in terms of semantic concepts are discussed below, as abstractive rationales:

Abstractive Rationales   In the NLP literature, abstractive rationales typically consist of concepts (Bashier et al., 2020; Jeblee et al., 2018), logical or linguistic structures (Hu et al., 2016), or human-readable free text (Forrest et al., 2018; Marasović et al., 2020). Free-text explanations have the advantage that they are accessible to anyone, but explanations presented in a formal language are unambiguous, typically easier to generate, and often more faithful. Sen et al. (2020), who present a neural rule-based approach to sentence classification, argue that first-order logic rules are also easily interpretable, and are sufficiently expressive to capture complex explanations.

The free-text explanations in Marasović et al. (2020) and the first order logic rules in Sen et al. (2020) are simply lists of propositions. Reiter (2019) argues this is insufficient. He lists four challenges of providing useful free-text explanations: human rationales are normally written with a purpose in mind. The quality of the explanation is to a large extent determined by whether it enables readers to grasp or follow the explanation with respect to its purpose. Human rationales are also written for particular audiences. Moreover, explanations are often more than just lists of facts; they often exhibit narrative and argumentative structure. Finally, human rationales ex-

Explanations	Form	Evaluation Strategies
Extractive rationales	highlights, heatmaps	heuristics, annotation, in-the-loop
Abstractive rationales	concepts, rules, text	annotation, in-the-loop
Training instances	examples	heuristics
Model visualizations	pictures	in-the-loop

Figure 11.1: Flavors of explanations.

press varying degrees of certainty. Reiter (2019) argues that all of these four characteristics are challenging to integrate in machine-generated free-text rationales.

Training Instances Explanations can also be a set or a ranked list of training examples: the decision to classify a review as positive, can be explained in terms of the words and phrases used in that review; but also in terms of the documents that led the learned model to induce positive polarity from these patterns. Exactly computing which training instances were most influential is computationally expensive, so sometimes explanations in terms of training instances sometimes rely on a subset of data, e.g., *prototypical* training instances or the training instances that are closest to the current example in an off-line text similarity space. Training instances are generally evaluated using heuristics. Feng and Boyd-Graber (2019) show that explanations in terms of training instances can complement extractive rationales in a real-world use case.

Model Visualizations Very few deep neural models can be comprehended holistically if printed on a piece of paper; most linear models or decision trees can be difficult to grasp this way. Nevertheless it sometimes make sense to visualize models or model components, or approximations thereof (say, through uptraining or knowledge distillation, both described in Chapter 10).

Human Explanations While we, as humans, often find it hard to provide a rationale for our impulses and judgments (Nisbett and Wilson, 1977), we often ask for and expect there are rationales behind the decisions of others. Such rationales can take the form of pointing to parts of the input: think, for example, of a school teacher highlighting grammatical errors in a student essay as a rationale for their grading of it. They can also take the form of logic rules, e.g., when a philosopher rejects their colleague's thesis; they can amount to mere reference to abstract concepts, e.g, classifying a novel as romantic because it is about love; or they can take the form of a full-fledged narrative (Reiter, 2019). The only one of the above forms of explanation that humans generally do *not* use is model visualization: we generally do not draw visualizations of our brains or approximations thereof as explanations of our decisions.

I list of the different flavors of explanation in Figure 11.1. Each flavor is associated with different evaluation strategies. I discuss heuristic evaluations (§11.2), evaluations against human gold-standard annotations (§11.3), as well as various forms of live experiments with human participants (§11.4), below.

11.2 HEURISTICS

Transformations   Some researchers have shown that some interpretability methods have unwanted properties, e.g., that they are easily fooled. Kindermans et al. (2017), for example, show that gradient-based functions (Chapter 9) are sensitive to constant shifts that do not affect model output. Shifts are simple transformations of existing datasets. Zhang et al. (2019) also discuss the vulnerability of gradient-based relevance attribution, but use adversarial training to learn such transformations. Similar observations have been made about other explainability methods: Alvarez-Melis and Jaakkola (2018), for example, discuss the sensitivity of LRP, Integrated Gradients, and LIME to Gaussian noise injection; Dombrowski et al. (2019) show how LRP, Integrated Gradients and several other algorithms are also sensitive to adversarial attacks.

Synthetic Datasets   It is often useful to explore the limits of explainability methods by creating synthetic datasets. All methods that provide explanations in the form of input mark-up (saliency maps) have a major limitation: they can only explain model decisions if some input regions are more related to the predicted class than others. Think, for example, of a recurrent architecture (e.g., an LSTM network) successfully trained to distinguish strings of odd length from strings of equal length. How would a gradient-based method explain any decision made by such a model, for example? The assumption that some input regions are more important than others, is called the linearity assumption in Jacovi and Goldberg (2020). This assumption is not discussed in their work, but the above example proves the linearity assumption is not always true.

○ **Open Problem**   How pervasive are violations of the linearity assumption in real-life NLP applications?

The idea of using synthetic datasets is also very related to the idea of using white-box models to evaluate explanations: if we know what happens inside a model, we can check if the explanations reflect this or not. That is, if we either hand-build a model that we can comprehend holistically, or design a synthetic dataset that is guaranteed to induce such a model, we can evaluate whether explainability methods produce rationales that explain their inner workings. Hao (2020), for example, uses white-box LSTMs to evaluate attribution methods.

Metrics for Extractive Rationales   A natural notion of the goodness of an extractive rationale—e.g., these k words are most important—is to quantify the degree to which it captures how $h(\mathbf{x}_i)$ changes in response to perturbations of $\mathbf{x}_i$ that, based on such a rationale, would remove some or all of the k most important words.

Ancona et al. (2018) present a heuristic metric called *sensitivity-n* that measure the correlation between a feature subset's estimated importance and the observed change in output when setting these features to 0. In an NLP context, this could, for example, be the correlation between the relevance attribution to a subset of k words and the observed change in output after removing those k words from the input.

Yeh et al. (2019) build on this work to propose a heuristic measure called *explanation infidelity*: instead of using the original input as baseline, they use random perturbations of the input; and they replace the correlation test with a proper loss function (mean square error). In an NLP context, this, for example, could be the cross-entropy between the model output after removing the above k words and the expected model output after removing k words randomly.

Adebayo et al. (2018) present two heuristics for evaluating extractive rationales. The so-called *model parameter randomization test* compares the extractive rationales of a trained model to the extractive rationales of a randomly initialized network. If the extractive rationales depend on the learned parameters, we would expect the rationales to differ. If the saliency method depends on the learned parameters of the model, we should expect its output to differ substantially between the two cases. The other heuristic, the so-called *data randomization test*, compares the rationales of the learned model with the rationales of a model trained on the same training dataset, but with randomly permuted labels (Bahdanau et al., 2015). Again, if the rationales are sensitive to input-output relations, the rationales of the two models should differ.

Note how the heuristic in Adebayo et al. (2018) differs from explanation infidelity in comparing the rationales of two models (rather than the output of one model across two examples). While explanation infidelity is perhaps more discriminatory, the methods in Adebayo et al. (2018) are perhaps more obviously adequate: if the rationales are not different under model parameter or data randomization, something is clearly wrong.

Carton et al. (2020) show, however, that human rationales are generally not in agreement with the heuristics used to evaluate relevance attribution in interpretability methods.

Metrics for Abstractive Rationales   Camburu et al. (2018) and Marasović et al. (2020) argue that standard n-gram-based automated metrics for text generation tasks are not sufficient for evaluating the plausibility of free-text abstractive rationales, since several rationales are typically valid without being paraphrases of one another. They instead rely on human judgments. Narang et al. (2020), however, report *both* human judgments and a standard metric from the machine translation literature. Abstractive rationales in the form of concepts or logic rules are more amenable for automated metrics, but human evaluations seem more common. Sen et al. (2020), for example, evaluate their logic rules in a human-in-the-loop experiment.

○ **Open Problem**   Can we design—or learn—robust automated metrics for abstractive rationales?

Metrics for Training Instances   Hanawa et al. (2020) discuss various heuristic metrics for evaluation explanations in terms of training instances: (a) the identical instance test, (b) the identical class test, (c) the top-k identical class test, and (d) the identical subclass test. The first two are sanity checks: (a) simply checks whether the most influential training data point x_j for a training data point x_i is x_i itself $(i = j)$. (b) checks whether the most influential training data point x_j for a *test* data point x_i is of the same class $(y_i = y_j)$. Next, (c) requires the same to hold true for the k most relevant training data points. Finally, (d) is only relevant for hierarchical classification problems and further stipulates that x_j and x_i should also share their subclasses. There is no evaluation of whether these heuristics are valid and capture human intuitions about relevance. It is not immediately clear why training instances should always be the most influential data points for their own classification by neural networks. Depending on how the network was initialized, some training instances have maybe never led to updates, but even if we abstract away from the initialization, some training instances may simply be redundant. Basu et al. (2021) use retrained networks, leaving out training data points, to obtain ground truths for evaluating influence functions. It is an open problem whether unbiased heuristics exist that approximate exact influence across initializations.

○ **Open Problem**   Can we design heuristics that estimate true influence across random initializations of our networks?

11.3   HUMAN ANNOTATIONS

We briefly review some of the human annotations for evaluating rationales, but provide a more extensive list of resources in §13.2. Søgaard et al. (2013) present human annotations of relevant (discontinuous) text spans across two document classification tasks: answer relevance and aspect-based sentiment analysis. The data has never been used to evaluate extractive rationales. Camburu et al. (2018) present human annotations of a natural language inference data set. Compared to Søgaard et al. (2013), their annotations highlighted single words, not discontinuous phrases. This means the data is not useful for evaluating hierarchical extractive rationales (Chen et al., 2020; Murdoch et al., 2018).

○ **Open Problem**   How do methods for generating hierarchical extractive rationales compare?

Rei and Søgaard (2018) show how to use multi-level annotations in existing NLP datasets for evaluating extractive rationales. They consider two sentence classification tasks: sentiment analysis and grammatical error detection. A similar experiment was performed for sentiment analysis in Bastings et al. (2019).

○ **Open Problem**   Can we leverage other NLP datasets with multi-level annotations for evaluating explanations?

Meanwhile, more human annotations of rationales have become available: ERASER (DeYoung et al., 2020) present a collection of such datasets, including the one presented in Camburu et al. (2018). They also cover sentiment analysis, machine reading, fact checking, etc. Other datasets include one for the task of detecting personal attacks in Wikipedia revision histories (Carton et al., 2018), one for aspect-based sentiment analysis (of beer reviews) discussed in Bastings et al. (2019), one for algebra word problems (Upadhyay and Chang, 2017), as well as a few datasets for machine reading or question answering (Lamm et al., 2020; Lee et al., 2020).

In both comparison with human annotations, and other types of experiments with human participants (see §11.4), it is important to consider the impact of how saliency maps are presented. Obviously, user interfaces can affect inference time, but I also want to point out a technical challenge: naive saliency maps are, in conjunction with *some* local attribution methods, sensitive to simple shifts of the data (Kindermans et al., 2017). Multiplying by the input, for example, can cause this to happen, because the input shift is carried through to the final attribution. If using such methods, this has to be corrected for in how the saliency maps are extracted.

11.4 HUMAN EXPERIMENTS

Human Forward Prediction   You fully understand something when you can predict its behavior. By the same token, obtaining explanations of the inner workings of a neural network should make its behavior more predictable to us. This is the idea behind human forward prediction (Gonzalez and Søgaard, 2020; Hase and Bansal, 2020; Nguyen, 2018): seeing a sample of good rationales should make it easier to predict the model's behavior on unseen data points. We can therefore evaluate explanation methods by average human performance when assisted by rationales generated by these methods.

Most NLP papers on human forward prediction (Gonzalez and Søgaard, 2020; Hase and Bansal, 2020; Nguyen, 2018) evaluate extractive rationales only. Feng and Boyd-Graber (2019) present a combination of extractive rationales and training instances. Alqaraawi et al. (2020) argue more categorically that, at least in the context of computer vision, it is not possible to reach a solid understanding of the inner workings of a deep neural network with the sole use of saliency-based explanations (extractive rationales).

◯ **Open Problem**   What explanations are more useful for human forward prediction across tasks: extractive or abstractive rationales, training instances, or model visualizations?

Rater Studies   A simpler alternative to human forward prediction experiments is human rater studies. Generally, rater studies involve choosing a system over another in the presence of explanations; this is a simpler task for human participants than *predicting the output* of a system. Ribeiro et al. (2016) presented two rater studies of LIME. In one of them, given two classifiers, participants were asked to choose which they believed would generalize better. In the second experiment, participants were asked to improve the accuracy of the classifier by removing features that do not seem to generalize. Unfortunately, both studies lacked significance testing and proper baselining by comparing with a condition in which no explanations were provided to participants. Lamm et al. (2020) provides another example of rater study evaluation in NLP.

Real-World Use Cases   The above experiments with human participants are either performed in the lab or on crowdsourcing platforms. Some authors have argued that such evaluations introduce an unfortunate bias (Buçinca et al., 2020; Gonzalez et al., 2020). While there is perhaps a continuum between the above experiments and *real-world* or *in-the-wild* evaluations, suffering from such biases to different degrees, some researchers have striven to simulate actual employment scenarios as much as possible.

Feng and Boyd-Graber (2019), for example, present an experiment in which participants in QuizBowl are assisted by an question answering model. The model can assist in three ways: (a) by presenting a list of predictions, along with confidence scores; (b) by presenting related training data points (in their case, by nearest neighbor search); and (c) by highlighting relevant input words (in their case, by elastic search). They sample a player's condition from the space of all possible combinations of these three methods and evaluate the impact of each method on human (machine-assisted) performance. Gonzalez et al. (2020) present a similar experiment in the context of voice assistants for open-domain question answering. Adebayo et al. (2020) presents experiments in using extractive rationales (from a total of 15 local explanation methods) for model debugging and show that the rationales are useful for identifying spurious correlations, but much less useful for identifying mislabeled training examples.

It is important to note that the arguments against human forward prediction and similar human-in-the-loop evaluations put forward in Buçinca et al. (2020), are based on the empirical observation that predictability does not correlate with the usefulness of rationales for other decision-making tasks. One weakness of their experimental design, however, is that they did not provide participants in their human forward prediction (proxy task) condition with training instances to learn model behavior. The importance of including such a training stage in human forward prediction experiments is discussed at length in Hase and Bansal (2020) and Gonzalez et al. (2020).

Bansal et al. (2021) further argues for the importance of *when* users are presented with model predictions and explanations. This information is typically presented to human participants before they are given a chance to reflect on their own, leading humans to perhaps rely too heavily on the model. On the other hand, Gonzalez and Søgaard (2020) show that explanations can speed up human inference if presented in advance.

○ **Open Problem**   How do we design experimental protocols for human evaluation of explanations based on training instances?

CHAPTER 12

Perspectives

Part of the motivation behind a taxonomy of machine learning methods is that it enables us to say something general about classes of methods, even about unseen members of these classes, i.e., methods that we are not aware of or that will be proposed in the future. §12.1 presents a few observations that hold for all members of different classes of the taxonomy presented here. §12.2 discusses a few things that I did not cover in the taxonomy presented here.

12.1 GENERAL OBSERVATIONS

Throughout this book I already discussed various observations about interpretability methods and how they relate. One example is the following observation.

Observation 12.1 Local methods *can* be applied globally,[1] whereas global methods *cannot* be applied locally.

In this section, I present additional observations that I believe are important to keep in mind when thinking coherently about explainable NLP. Here's a first example:

Observation 12.2 Local backward methods are always attribution methods (presenting feature summary statistics).

Since local interpretability methods have to provide explanations in terms of input or output (because they do not modify model weights), and since backward passes do not generate output distributions, they have to present explanations in terms of attribution of relevance or gradients to input features or input segments.

The next observation I would like to make here relates to the notion of the *faithfulness* of model explanations. Faithfulness is a commonly used term in several areas of NLP, including abstractive summarization and machine translation, but here it refers to whether the output of such models is semantically coherent with the input. This is *not* what I mean here. Faithful explanations refer to explanations that adequate account for the inner workings of the models they explain. In the words of Jacovi and Goldberg (2020), *a faithful interpretation is one that accurately represents the reasoning process behind the model's prediction.*

Faithfulness has been a key discussion point in recent literature on explainable NLP (Jacovi and Goldberg, 2020), as well as more generally in machine learning (Le Merrer and Trédan,

---

[1]See Ribeiro et al. (2016) for how to do this with LIME, for example.

2020). I argue that in some sense, only global methods can be unfaithful. This may sound surprising at first, given that the literature on faithfulness has focused mostly on local methods.[2] My point, however, is that previous discussions often conflate the idea that an explanation is unfaithful and situations where an explanation is simply misinterpreted. While the contribution of local methods have often been misunderstood or overestimated, the local methods in some sense just do what they do. Global methods can, however, easily be *misleading*.

Gradients represent gradients, gates represent gates, attention heads represent attention heads, etc. None of these represent reasoning in a sense that would satisfy a philosopher, but they all represent aspects of what models are doing. Do they represent reasoning in a sense that we care about when explaining NLP models? Of course they do. When explaining NLP models we are interested in how they operate. Gradients, gates, attention heads, etc., are model components that influence model output. They are meaningful objects of explanation, but they do what they do. They cannot be unfaithful: gradients reflect what gradients do, gates reflect what gates do, attention heads reflect what attention heads do, etc. In summary, none of the local methods can be unfaithful.

Observation 12.3   Only global methods can be unfaithful.

Local methods compute quantities based on forward or backward passes, but these quantities are not induced to simulate anything. Global methods induce parameters to simulate a distribution and can be more or less faithful to this distribution, but since local methods simply 'read off' their quantities, they cannot be unfaithful. Only, the quantities can be misinterpreted by those who wish to use them for downstream applications.[3]

Observation 12.4   Global methods can at best be epsilon-faithful and only on i.i.d. instances.

Definition 1.1 explicates how global methods rely on inductions from representative samples.[4] Since their faithfulness is the inverse of the empirical risk of these inductions, it follows

---

[2]Ribeiro et al. (2016), for example, presents a local explainability method, yet explicitly discusses its faithfulness. Its faithfulness is also discussed in Lundberg and Lee (2017), for example. The method, which is called LIME, presented in their paper *does* initially look like an exception to my discussion above. Is this an exception to the above observation? In Chapter 9, in which I discussed LIME, it was discussed at some length, whether the method is in fact local or global; it is in some ways similar to global methods. The two discussions are related: LIME seems like a method that can be unfaithful, *because* it, in some ways, is similar to global methods. In Chapter 9, I argue that LIME is a local method, because the induction of the linear approximation of the model's decision boundary is based on random perturbations of the input example, not an actual sample of observations. The fact that a learning algorithm is used to derive the linear approximation does not mean the approximation is *learned* in any real sense of the word: the approximation can be more or less tight, but not unfaithful.

[3]LIME (Ribeiro et al., 2016), a local uptraining method, presents an interesting borderline case. Ribeiro et al. (2016) explicitly discuss the faithfulness of LIME, directly contradicting Observation 5.2. We argue their discussion is misleading. While LIME uses a learning algorithm (e.g., logistic regression) to estimate a linear approximation of the model decision boundary around a single example, they do not induce this approximation from a sample of data, but random perturbations of the example. This is merely an efficient way of approximating an expensive model decomposition and can therefore not be unfaithful, but merely a more or less tight approximation.

[4]However, NLP data samples are rarely *i.i.d.* (Søgaard et al., 2021). If samples are not representative, ϵ is unbounded (Wolpert, 1996), and we can therefore conclude that global methods are always potentially misleading on specific data points.

that global methods can at best be ϵ-faithful, with ϵ the expected loss of these inductions. Note that when the explanation is a model approximation θ', $\epsilon = \mathbb{E}[\ell(\theta(x), \theta'(x))]$.

Observation 12.5   Only forward methods can be used for local layer-wise analysis.

Several papers compare representations at different layers to better understand the dynamics of deep neural networks in the context of individual examples (Abdou et al., 2019). Since local backward methods are always attribution methods (Observation 5.1), and layer-wise analysis concerns differences between layers, local backward methods cannot be used for local layer-wise, simply because they only output attributions at the input level.

Observation 12.6   No equivalence relations can hold across the four categories, e.g., between local and global methods, or forward and backward ones.

This is perhaps a trivial observation in the context of a taxonomy, but it shows the value of having a taxonomy: several equivalence results have been presented in the literature (Ancona et al., 2018; Samek et al., 2021), e.g., between configurations of layer-wise relevance propagation (using LRP-0 at every layer) and deep Taylor decomposition (Montavon et al., 2017), or between DeepLift (Shrikumar et al., 2017) and integrated gradients (Mudrakarta et al., 2018; Sundararajan et al., 2017) (to be precise, DeepLift approximates integrated gradients). By consistently classifying approaches in our taxonomy, we effectively prune the search space of possible equivalences.

Observation 12.7   Local methods can always characterize models globally on i.i.d. samples.

See Ribeiro et al. (2016) for how to do this with LIME. It should be easy to see how this result generalizes to all other local methods.
Other observations relate to the form of explanations.

Observation 12.8   All methods that return extractive rationales can only explain decisions in terms of tokens or features *present* in the input, but not in terms of tokens or features *absent* from the input (Dhurandhar et al., 2018). Furthermore, sometimes explanations are not about the presence or absence of input tokens or features, but about how they relate, or add up.

To see (i), think of how explaining why good sentiment models label some sentences as *neutral*, for example, is more about the absence of polarity words than about the presence of any other words. Limitation (ii) shows up, for example, when explaining the decisions of a model trained to detect sentences with more digits and punctuation than letters. Such a model would pay equal attention to all characters in a sentence, and a highlighting of the most important tokens or features would not really provide us with *any* explanation of the inner workings of the model. The methods to which this applies, are *limited by the expressivity of extractive rationales*.

These limitations follow simply from the fact that extractive rationales are extractive, i.e., sub-sets of the input tokens or features, but note that the limitation is coherent with the taxonomy presented in this book.

Another observation relates only to local methods. Many local methods are attribution methods that produce highlighting or heat maps of our input examples, but this does not hold for all local methods. Counter-examples are word association norms, word analogies, concept activation, fill-in-the-gap probes, etc. Note that these methods are all local-forward explanations of continuous output (Chapter 7) or discrete output (Chapter 9). This makes intuitive sense: local explanations are either in terms of the input or the output of a model, since these are the what we, as end users, relate to.

Observation 12.9   Of the local methods, only explanations of continuous or discrete output provide explanations that are *not* extractive rationales.

Most of these methods provide explanations that are akin to traditional error analysis based on test suites or cherry picking, and some provide explanations in terms of training instances.

Here is an observation about evaluations of explanations: heuristic evaluations for extrac-tive rationales, e.g., looking at output change from removing relevant or random words, do not apply to abstractive rationales or explanations in terms of training instances. This is because these heuristics are designed to probe the importance of the input tokens or features that are attributed relevance in the extractive rationale. On the other hand, the heuristics used to eval-uate explanations in terms of training instances, e.g., whether a training data point is assigned influence for its own classification, are not applicable to extractive or abstractive rationales.

Observation 12.10   Evaluation heuristics apply to extractive rationales or training instances, but not to both.

Our final observation relates to the possibility of layer-wise analysis. Several papers have engaged in layer-wise analysis of NLP models, e.g., Abdou et al. (2019); Ravishankar et al. (2021); Tenney et al. (2019), performing comparisons of representations at different layers of these models. Tenney et al. (2019) use probing classifiers (Chapter 8) to obtain such an analysis, while Abdou et al. (2019) uses representational similarity analysis (Chapter 8), and Ravishankar et al. (2021) uses attention flow (Chapter 5). In fact, almost all the methods covered in this book can be used to perform such layer-wise, comparative analysis. Only exceptions seem to be explanations of discrete output.[5]

Observation 12.11   All methods, except explanations of discrete output, can be used for layer-wise comparative analysis.

---

[5]Obtaining discrete output from hidden layers would amount to training auxiliary probing classifiers.

12.2   BEYOND TAXONOMY

In this section, I discuss a few topics the taxonomy presented here does not cover, and that are orthogonal to the distinctions made in it.

Contrastive Explanations   The terms of *contrastive* and *comparative* are easily conflated, but in explainable NLP, the former term seems to refer to methods that either reason about the impact of the presence *and* absence of input features, or reason about the impact of the presence of input features given alternative labelings, while comparative analyses perform model or layer-wise comparisons. Contrastive analyses thus pertain to local methods, whereas both local and global methods can be relevant for comparative analyses.

In a contrastive analysis of a local decision, we are interested in which parts of the input should be minimally present, and what other features or input tokens should be minimally absent, for the model to make the decision it made. The key insight here is that while some features make positive contributions, other (absent) features could have perhaps overruled these. In other words, a decision may be explained by the absence of absent features.

How do you reason about what absent features are relevant for a decision? Dhurandhar et al. (2018), albeit in the context of computer vision, relies on an autoencoder to generate candidate features; the architecture is similar to causal local uptraining methods (Chapter 9). In Jacovi and Goldberg (2020), the term *contrastive* refers to attributing relevance to input tokens for a particular decision, *baselined* by what would have been relevant for an alternative decision. A better term for this is perhaps *counterfactual* explanations, the term used in Mothilal et al. (2020).

Comparative Explanations   As just argued for in §12.1, most of the methods discussed in this book can be used to compare two models or two layers in a deep neural network. It seems the only exceptions here are explanations of discrete output (local or global), which can of course be used to compare different models, but not different layers. For example, Abdou et al. (2019) use representational similarity analysis (Chapter 8) to compare the geometry of representations in different language models and different layers of these language models. While such comparisons can be performed in different ways, associated with different experimental protocols, I have ignored these questions here, as they are completely orthogonal to my taxonomy of explanation methods.

Method Combination   In the above I discussed explainability methods in isolation, except for briefly mentioning that two-stage methods (Ramamurthy et al., 2020; Ribeiro et al., 2018; Sushil et al., 2018) exist (Chapter 1). I also mentioned the human-in-the-loop evaluation presented in Fu et al. (2020), which also included conditions in which participants were presented with both extractive rationales and training instances. Olah et al. (2018), however, treat all of these methods as building blocks for creating rich interfaces. This is a very interesting research direction that I, alas, will not discuss in this book.

12.3   MORAL FOUNDATIONS OF EXPLANATIONS

Explainable NLP is often motivated by the premise that humans have a *right to explanation*: if their life is in some way affected by NLP models, they should want to and be able to query for the rationale behind the decisions of those models. There are many other motivations, such as error analysis, model maintenance, more efficient computing, and detection of vulnerabilities against adversarial attacks, but perhaps the most cited motivation, especially for local explanation methods, is the right to explanation.

Goodman and Flaxman (2017) point out how the EU's General Data Protection Regulation (GDPR) and other regulations is an opportunity for researchers to explore explainability techniques such as those discussed in the above. Others (Wachter et al., 2017) have questioned whether GDPR *does* give people a *right to explanation*, or in what sense it does.

It is interesting to think about where the right to explanation would come from, from a moral perspective. Zerilli et al. (2018), for example, worry that automated decision-making is being held to an unrealistically high standard. Are we really, they ask, asking for the same degree of transparency from human decision-makers? The reviewability of decisions made by lower courts, tribunals, and administrative agencies is a key feature of modern democracies, of course, and even students can typically ask for the rationale behind their teachers' grading of their essays. What Zerilli et al. (2018) argue, though, is that *if human decision-making represents the gold standard for transparency, we think AI can in some respects already be said to meet it.* The explanations that we typically ask human decision-makers for *do not yield the entrails of a decision, or illuminate the cognitive processes leading to its conclusion.* These processes are *not* transparent, often not even to the decision makers themselves.

Say, for example, that after reading 12 chapters of this book you come to the conclusion you do not like it. As a consequence, you decide *not* to cite it or *not* to recommend it to your students or peers. Why did you arrive at that conclusion? You may not like the language in which it is written, you may feel it fails to discuss relevant work, or you may disagree with specific arguments I made. Either of the above would provide a *rationale*. Now say your reason for not liking the book is that I failed to include your favorite paper on explainable NLP. This seems like an explanation at first, but why is this your favorite paper, and how come you think it should be included in this book? And how did you come to think of that in the first place? Your ability to recall this paper while reading my book, likely depends on how you brain organizes such information, which in turn depends on your experience with organizing and retrieving such information, the extent of which you are hardly cognizant of. It would there be a bit of an uphill battle to provide a full account of the processes that led you to your conclusion that you do not like this book.

Note that the literature on explainable NLP and machine learning typically assumes that human decision-making is, in principle, fully transparent: Mittelstadt et al. (2016), for example, states that *algorithmic processing contrasts with traditional decision-making, where human decision-makers can in principle articulate their rationale when queried, limited only by their desire and capacity to give an explanation, and the questioner's capacity to understand it.* I tend to think that, on the contrary, while human decision-making is largely black-boxed (for now), we have come a long way in understanding the dynamics of neural networks; while much work remains, and current methods have clear limitations—leading to misleading global explanations, useless local explanations, and such—the problem of understanding the processes involved in neural network decisions is near-trivial compared to the problem of understanding the processes involved in human decisions.

CHAPTER 13

Resources

13.1 CODE

There exists a wide range of libraries and code bases for explainability methods already, but many of them overlap in what they cover. Here is a list of libraries that I have used or that seemed relevant to me, with a slight bias toward Python, and trying to avoid too much overlap. I apologize in advance for all the amazing toolkits I left out.

ACE Tensorflow code for Ghorbani et al. (2019). See https://github.com/amiratag/ACE.

AIX360 Python library with implementations of LIME (Ribeiro et al., 2016) and contrastive explanation (Dhurandhar et al., 2018), among other algorithms. See https://github.com/Trusted-AI/AIX360.

Alibi Explain Python toolkit for integrated gradients, contrastive, and counterfactual explanations. See https://docs.seldon.io/projects/alibi/en/stable/.

AllenInterpret Library built on top of AllenNLP, with a focus on gradient-based saliency maps and adversarial attacks; described in Wallace et al. (2019). See https://allennlp.org/interpret.

BertViz BertViz (Vig, 2019) is a popular visualization tool for attention (Chapter 5) in language models. It is available at https://github.com/jessevig/bertviz.

Captum.ai The PyTorch library Captum (Kokhlikyan et al., 2020) is available at https://captum.ai/ and supports integrated gradients for most neural architectures relevant to NLP.

Dalex Library for interpretability, bias, and fairness, described in Biecek (2018); includes LIME, for example. See https://dalex.drwhy.ai/python/api/.

Darkon Library for influence functions and gradience-based explanations. See https://darkon.readthedocs.io.

DeepLift Keras/Tensorflow implementation of DeepLift. See https://github.com/kundajelab/deeplift.

DiCE Code base for counterfactual explanations (Mothilal et al., 2020). See https://github.com/interpretml/DiCE.

ExBert   The ExBert tool (Hoover et al., 2020) is a visualization fool for transformer architectures and available at https://github.com/bhoov/exbert.

LIT   The LIT tool (Tenney et al., 2020) provides an implementation of and interface to several local explanation methods, including attention, vanilla gradients, and LIME.

LRP for LSTMs   The code from Arras et al. (2017) (see Chapter 3). See https://github.com/ArrasL/LRP_for_LSTM.

LRP Toolbox   The LRP Toolbox (Lapuschkin et al., 2016) provides simple and accessible stand-alone implementations of layer-wise relevance propagation for deep neural networks in Caffe, supporting Matlab and Python. See the project Github at https://github.com/sebastian-lapuschkin/lrp_toolbox.

LSTMVis   The LSTMVis tool (Strobelt et al., 2017) visualizes gates in recurrent neural networks. See http://lstm.seas.harvard.edu/.

Lucid   Tensorflow library for compositing interfaces combining multiple explanation methods. The library is available at https://github.com/tensorflow/lucid.

iNNvestigate   Keras library described in Alber et al. (2019); comes with implementations of a range of methods for local explanations of training dynamics (Chapter 3), including guided backpropagation, Deep Taylor decomposition, layer-wise relevance propagation, etc. See https://github.com/albermax/innvestigate.

mPerturb   PyTorch implementation of Fong and Vedaldi (2017), deriving explanations from data perturbations. See https://github.com/ajsanjoaquin/mPerturb.

NeuroX   A library for ablation of individual neurons, described in Dalvi et al. (2018). See https://github.com/fdalvi/NeuroX.

PathExplain   Code from Janizek et al. (2020), improving explanations from integrated gradients. See https://github.com/suinleelab/path_explain.

TCAV   Code from Kim et al. (2018). See https://github.com/tensorflow/tcav.

TextBrewer   The TextBrewer toolkit (Yang et al., 2020) facilitates setting up distillation experiments. See https://github.com/airaria/TextBrewer.

TransformerAnatomy   Code for Jo and Myaeng (2020), i.e., visualization of attention heads. See https://github.com/heartcored98/transformer_anatomy.

Word2Viz   Online tool for visualizing word analogies. See https://lamyiowce.github.io/word2viz/.

13.2 DATASETS AND BENCHMARKS

In Chapter 11, I briefly discussed the use of human annotations for evaluating extractive and abstractive rationales. Here is a list of interesting benchmark datasets for different NLP tasks. See also Wiegreffe and Marasović (2021).

AQUA-RAT Dataset for algebra solving with explanations, discussed in Ling et al. (2017). See https://www.kaggle.com/jeromeblanchet/aquarat-algebra-question-answering-with-rationale.

ATOMIC The ATOMIC knowledge graph (Sap et al., 2019) for querying for common sense patterns in language models. See https://mosaickg.apps.allenai.org/kg_atomic.

BeerAdvocate Aspect-based sentiment analysis dataset, with two-level annotations, used in several explainable NLP papers (Bastings et al., 2019; Søgaard et al., 2013). See https://snap.stanford.edu/data/web-BeerAdvocate.html.

ERASER The ERASER benchmark (DeYoung et al., 2020) is available at https://www.eraserbenchmark.com/. It comprises several NLP datasets with explanations, including for sentiment analysis and natural language inference.

EQUATE The EQUATE benchmark (Ravichander et al., 2019) probes the sensitivity of NLP models to numerical reasoning (see Chapter 9).

Evidence Inference Dataset for medical QA with explanations. See https://evidence-inference.ebm-nlp.com/blog/.

Explainaboard Platform for analysis based on downstream evaluation, discussed in Fu et al. (2020). See http://explainaboard.nlpedia.ai/.

Explanation Bank Multihop question answering resource with explanations, discussed in Xie et al. (2020). See http://cognitiveai.org/explanationbank/.

QED Structured rationale annotations for question answering, described in Lamm et al. (2020). See https://github.com/google-research-datasets/QED.

SciFact Dataset for fact checking with explanations, discussed in Wadden et al. (2020). See https://github.com/allenai/scifact.

Stanford Sentiment Treebank Multi-level sentiment analysis annotations used in several explainable NLP papers (Bastings et al., 2019; Rei and Søgaard, 2018). See https://nlp.stanford.edu/sentiment/treebank.html.

VCR   Dataset for visual commonsense reading with explanations, discussed in Zellers et al. (2019). See https://visualcommonsense.com/.

WIQA   The What-If QA dataset is available at https://allenai.org/data/wiqa.

Bibliography

Mostafa Abdou, Artur Kulmizev, Felix Hill, Daniel M. Low, and Anders Søgaard. 2019. Higher-order comparisons of sentence encoder representations. In *Proc. of the 2019 Conference on Empirical Methods in Natural Language Processing and the 9th International Joint Conference on Natural Language Processing (EMNLP-IJCNLP)*, pages 5838–5845, Hong Kong, China. Association for Computational Linguistics. DOI: 10.18653/v1/d19-1593. 43, 65, 66, 67

Mostafa Abdou, Artur Kulmizev, Vinit Ravishankar, Lasha Abzianidze, and Johan Bos. 2018. What can we learn from semantic tagging? In *Proc. of the 2018 Conference on Empirical Methods in Natural Language Processing*, pages 4881–4889, Brussels, Belgium. Association for Computational Linguistics. DOI: 10.18653/v1/d18-1526. 28

Samira Abnar, Lisa Beinborn, Rochelle Choenni, and Willem Zuidema. 2019. Blackbox meets blackbox: Representational similarity & stability analysis of neural language models and brains. In *Proc. of the 2019 ACL Workshop BlackboxNLP: Analyzing and Interpreting Neural Networks for NLP*, pages 191–203, Florence, Italy. Association for Computational Linguistics. DOI: 10.18653/v1/W19-4820. 43

Samira Abnar and Willem Zuidema. 2020. Quantifying attention flow in transformers. In *Proc. of the 58th Annual Meeting of the Association for Computational Linguistics*, pages 4190–4197, Online. Association for Computational Linguistics. DOI: 10.18653/v1/2020.acl-main.385. 5, 10, 12, 15, 18, 32, 33, 34

Amina Adadi and Mohammed Berrada. 2018. Peeking inside the black-box: A survey on explainable artificial intelligence (xai). *IEEE Access*, 6:52138–52160. DOI: 10.1109/access.2018.2870052. 4, 7, 8

Julius Adebayo, Justin Gilmer, Michael Muelly, Ian Goodfellow, Moritz Hardt, and Been Kim. 2018. Sanity checks for saliency maps. In *Advances in Neural Information Processing Systems*, volume 31. Curran Associates, Inc. 59

Julius Adebayo, Michael Muelly, Ilaria Liccardi, and Been Kim. 2020. Debugging tests for model explanations. In *NeurIPS*. 62

Roee Aharoni and Yoav Goldberg. 2020. Unsupervised domain clusters in pretrained language models. In *Proc. of the 58th Annual Meeting of the Association for Computational Linguistics*, pages 7747–7763, Online. Association for Computational Linguistics. DOI: 10.18653/v1/2020.acl-main.692. 5, 44

G. Alain and Yoshua Bengio. 2017. Understanding intermediate layers using linear classifier probes. In *ICLR*. 44

Maximilian Alber, Sebastian Lapuschkin, Philipp Seegerer, Miriam Hägele, Kristof T. Schütt, Grégoire Montavon, Wojciech Samek, Klaus-Robert Müller, Sven Dähne, and Pieter-Jan Kindermans. 2019. innvestigate neural networks! *Journal of Machine Learning Research*, 20(93):1–8. 72

Afra Alishahi, Grzegorz Chrupala, and Tal Linzen. 2019. Analyzing and interpreting neural networks for nlp: A report on the first blackboxnlp workshop. *Natural Language Engineering*, 25(4):543–557. 2018 EMNLP BlackboxNLP : Analyzing and Interpreting Neural Networks for NLP ; Conference date: 01-11-2018 Through 01-11-2018. DOI: 10.1017/s135132491900024x. 1

Ahmed Alqaraawi, Martin Schuessler, Philipp Weiß, Enrico Costanza, and Nadia Berthouze. 2020. Evaluating saliency map explanations for convolutional neural networks: A user study. In *Proc. of the 25th International Conference on Intelligent User Interfaces*, IUI '20, pages 275–285, New York, NY, Association for Computing Machinery. DOI: 10.1145/3377325.3377519. 61

David Alvarez-Melis and Tommi Jaakkola. 2017. A causal framework for explaining the predictions of black-box sequence-to-sequence models. In *Proc. of the 2017 Conference on Empirical Methods in Natural Language Processing*, pages 412–421, Copenhagen, Denmark. Association for Computational Linguistics. DOI: 10.18653/v1/d17-1042. 12, 20, 45, 51

David Alvarez-Melis and Tommi S. Jaakkola. 2018. On the robustness of interpretability methods. In *2018 ICML Workshop on Human Interpretability in Machine Learning (WHI 2018)*, Stockholm, Sweden. 58

Marco Ancona, Enea Ceolini, Cengiz Öztireli, and Markus Gross. 2018. Towards better understanding of gradient-based attribution methods for deep neural networks. In *International Conference on Learning Representations*. 24, 58, 65

Andrea Apicella, Francesco Isgrò, Roberto Prevete, and Guglielmo Tamburrini. 2020. Middle-level features for the explanation of classification systems by sparse dictionary methods. *Int. J. Neural Syst.*, 30(8):2050040:1–2050040:17. DOI: 10.1142/s0129065720500409. 29

Leila Arras, Franziska Horn, Grégoire Montavon, Klaus-Robert Müller, and Wojciech Samek. 2016. Explaining predictions of non-linear classifiers in NLP. In *Proc. of the 1st Workshop on Representation Learning for NLP*, pages 1–7, Berlin, Germany. Association for Computational Linguistics. DOI: 10.18653/v1/w16-1601. 5, 6, 12, 22

Leila Arras, Grégoire Montavon, Klaus-Robert Müller, and Wojciech Samek. 2017. Explaining recurrent neural network predictions in sentiment analysis. In *Proc. of the 8th Workshop on*

Computational Approaches to Subjectivity, Sentiment and Social Media Analysis, pages 159–168, Copenhagen, Denmark. Association for Computational Linguistics. DOI: 10.18653/v1/w17-5221. 22, 72

Leila Arras, Ahmed Osman, Klaus-Robert Müller, and Wojciech Samek. 2019. Evaluating recurrent neural network explanations. In *Proc. of the 2019 ACL Workshop BlackboxNLP: Analyzing and Interpreting Neural Networks for NLP*, pages 113–126, Florence, Italy. Association for Computational Linguistics. DOI: 10.18653/v1/w19-4813. 22

Pepa Atanasova, Jakob Grue Simonsen, Christina Lioma, and Isabelle Augenstein. 2020a. A diagnostic study of explainability techniques for text classification. In *Proc. of the 2020 Conference on Empirical Methods in Natural Language Processing (EMNLP)*, pages 3256–3274, Online. Association for Computational Linguistics. DOI: 10.18653/v1/2020.emnlp-main.263. 3, 10, 21

Pepa Atanasova, Jakob Grue Simonsen, Christina Lioma, and Isabelle Augenstein. 2020b. Generating fact checking explanations. In *Proc. of the 58th Annual Meeting of the Association for Computational Linguistics*, pages 7352–7364, Online. Association for Computational Linguistics. DOI: 10.18653/v1/2020.acl-main.656. 28

Kambiz Azarian, Yash Bhalgat, Jinwon Lee, and Tijmen Blankevoort. 2020. Learned threshold pruning. In *ICLR*. 28

Jimmy Ba and Rich Caruana. 2014. Do deep nets really need to be deep? In *Advances in Neural Information Processing Systems*, volume 27. Curran Associates, Inc. 53

Sebastian Bach, Alexander Binder, Grégoire Montavon, Frederick Klauschen, Klaus-Robert Müller, and Wojciech Samek. 2015. On pixel-wise explanations for non-linear classifier decisions by layer-wise relevance propagation. *PLoS ONE*, 10(7):e0130140. DOI: 10.1371/journal.pone.0130140. 12, 17

S. Bacher. 2012. Still not enough taxonomists: reply to joppa et al. *Trends in Ecology & Evolution*, 27 2:65–66. DOI: 10.1016/j.tree.2011.11.003. 1

Dzmitry Bahdanau, Kyunghyun Cho, and Yoshua Bengio. 2015. Neural machine translation by jointly learning to align and translate. In *ICLR*. 31, 32, 59

Gagan Bansal, Tongshuang Wu, Joyce Zhou, Raymond Fok, Besmira Nushi, Ece Kamar, Marco Túlio Ribeiro, and Daniel S. Weld. 2021. Does the whole exceed its parts? the effect of ai explanations on complementary team performance. *Proc. of the 2021 CHI Conference on Human Factors in Computing Systems*. DOI: 10.1145/3411764.3445717. 62

Housam Khalifa Bashier, Mi-Young Kim, and Randy Goebel. 2020. RANCC: Rationalizing neural networks via concept clustering. In *Proc. of the 28th International Conference on Computational Linguistics*, pages 3214–3224, Barcelona, Spain (Online). International Committee on Computational Linguistics. DOI: 10.18653/v1/2020.coling-main.286. 46, 56

Jasmijn Bastings, Wilker Aziz, and Ivan Titov. 2019. Interpretable neural predictions with differentiable binary variables. In *Proc. of the 57th Annual Meeting of the Association for Computational Linguistics*, pages 2963–2977, Florence, Italy. Association for Computational Linguistics. DOI: 10.18653/v1/p19-1284. 28, 60, 61, 73

Jasmijn Bastings and Katja Filippova. 2020. The elephant in the interpretability room: Why use attention as explanation when we have saliency methods? In *Proc. of the Third BlackboxNLP Workshop on Analyzing and Interpreting Neural Networks for NLP*, pages 149–155, Online. Association for Computational Linguistics. DOI: 10.18653/v1/2020.blackboxnlp-1.14. 32

Samyadeep Basu, Philip Pope, and Soheil Feizi. 2021. Influence functions in deep learning are fragile. ArXiv 2006.14651. 60

Samyadeep Basu, Xuchen You, and Soheil Feizi. 2020. On second-order group influence functions for black-box predictions. In *Proc. of the 37th International Conference on Machine Learning*, volume 119 of *Proc. of Machine Learning Research*, pages 715–724. PMLR. 51

J. Baxter. 2000. A model of inductive bias learning. *Journal of Artificial Intelligence Research*, 12:149–198. DOI: 10.1613/jair.731. 19

Yonatan Belinkov. 2021. Probing classifiers: Promises, shortcomings, and alternatives. ArXiv 2102.12452. 5, 12, 19, 45

Yonatan Belinkov, Lluís Màrquez, Hassan Sajjad, Nadir Durrani, Fahim Dalvi, and James Glass. 2017. Evaluating layers of representation in neural machine translation on part-of-speech and semantic tagging tasks. In *Proc. of the Eighth International Joint Conference on Natural Language Processing (Volume 1: Long Papers)*, pages 1–10, Taipei, Taiwan. Asian Federation of Natural Language Processing. 44

Gábor Berend. 2017. Sparse coding of neural word embeddings for multilingual sequence labeling. *Transactions of the Association for Computational Linguistics*, 5:247–261. DOI: 10.1162/tacl_a_00059. 29

Przemyslaw Biecek. 2018. Dalex: Explainers for complex predictive models in r. *Journal of Machine Learning Research*, 19(84):1–5. 71

Alexander Binder, Grégoire Montavon, Sebastian Bach, Klaus-Robert Müller, and Wojciech Samek. 2016. Layer-wise relevance propagation for neural networks with local renormalization layers. ArXiv 1604.00825. DOI: 10.1007/978-3-319-44781-0_8. 24

Joachim Bingel and Anders Søgaard. 2017. Identifying beneficial task relations for multi-task learning in deep neural networks. In *Proc. of the 15th Conference of the European Chapter of the Association for Computational Linguistics: Volume 2, Short Papers*, pages 164–169, Valencia, Spain. Association for Computational Linguistics. DOI: 10.18653/v1/e17-2026. 54

Steven Bramhall, Hayley Horn, Michael Tieu, and Nibhrat Lohia. 2020. Qlime-a quadratic local interpretable model-agnostic explanation approach. *SMU Data Science Review*, 3. 50, 51

Christopher Brix, Parnia Bahar, and Hermann Ney. 2020. Successfully applying the stabilized lottery ticket hypothesis to the transformer architecture. In *Proc. of the 58th Annual Meeting of the Association for Computational Linguistics*, pages 3909–3915, Online. Association for Computational Linguistics. DOI: 10.18653/v1/2020.acl-main.360. 27

Gino Brunner, Yang Liu, Damian Pascual, Oliver Richter, Massimiliano Ciaramita, and Roger Wattenhofer. 2020. On identifiability in transformers. In *International Conference on Learning Representations*. 32

Aakriti Budhraja, Madhura Pande, Preksha Nema, Pratyush Kumar, and Mitesh M. Khapra. 2020. On the weak link between importance and prunability of attention heads. In *Proc. of the 2020 Conference on Empirical Methods in Natural Language Processing (EMNLP)*, pages 3230–3235, Online. Association for Computational Linguistics. DOI: 10.18653/v1/2020.emnlp-main.260. 36, 37

Zana Buçinca, Phoebe Lin, Krzysztof Z. Gajos, and Elena L. Glassman. 2020. Proxy tasks and subjective measures can be misleading in evaluating explainable ai systems. *Proc. of the 25th International Conference on Intelligent User Interfaces*. DOI: 10.1145/3377325.3377498. 62

Jesús Calvillo and Matthew Crocker. 2018. Language production dynamics with recurrent neural networks. In *Proc. of the Eight Workshop on Cognitive Aspects of Computational Language Learning and Processing*, pages 17–26, Melbourne. Association for Computational Linguistics. DOI: 10.18653/v1/w18-2803. 23

Oana-Maria Camburu, Tim Rocktäschel, Thomas Lukasiewicz, and Phil Blunsom. 2018. e-snli: Natural language inference with natural language explanations. ArXiv 1812.01193. 59, 60, 61

Nicola De Cao, Michael Schlichtkrull, Wilker Aziz, and Ivan Titov. 2021. How do decisions emerge across layers in neural models? interpretation with differentiable masking. ArXiv 2004.14992. DOI: 10.18653/v1/2020.emnlp-main.262. 28

Samuel Carton, Qiaozhu Mei, and Paul Resnick. 2018. Extractive adversarial networks: High-recall explanations for identifying personal attacks in social media posts. In *Proc. of the 2018*

Conference on Empirical Methods in Natural Language Processing, pages 3497–3507, Brussels, Belgium. Association for Computational Linguistics. DOI: 10.18653/v1/d18-1386. 61

Samuel Carton, Anirudh Rathore, and Chenhao Tan. 2020. Evaluating and characterizing human rationales. In *Proc. of the 2020 Conference on Empirical Methods in Natural Language Processing (EMNLP)*, pages 9294–9307, Online. Association for Computational Linguistics. DOI: 10.18653/v1/2020.emnlp-main.747. 59

Rich Caruana. 1993. Multitask learning: A knowledge-based source of inductive bias. In *ICML*. DOI: 10.1016/b978-1-55860-307-3.50012-5. 19

D. V. Carvalho, E. M. Pereira, and Jaime S. Cardoso. 2019. Machine learning interpretability: A survey on methods and metrics. *Electronics*, 8:832. DOI: 10.3390/electronics8080832. 3, 4, 5, 7, 8, 25

Rui Chaves. 2020. What don't RNN language models learn about filler-gap dependencies? In *Proc. of the Society for Computation in Linguistics 2020*, pages 1–11, New York, New York. Association for Computational Linguistics. 49

Hila Chefer, Shir Gur, and Lior Wolf. 2020. Transformer interpretability beyond attention visualization. ArXiv 2012.09838. 23

Hanjie Chen, Guangtao Zheng, and Yangfeng Ji. 2020. Generating hierarchical explanations on text classification via feature interaction detection. In *Proc. of the 58th Annual Meeting of the Association for Computational Linguistics*, pages 5578–5593, Online. Association for Computational Linguistics. DOI: 10.18653/v1/2020.acl-main.494. 56, 60

Valerie Chen, Jeffrey Li, Joon Sik Kim, Gregory Plumb, and Ameet Talwalkar. 2021. Towards connecting use cases and methods in interpretable machine learning. ArXiv 2103.06254. 10

Kyunghyun Cho, Bart van Merriënboer, Caglar Gulcehre, Dzmitry Bahdanau, Fethi Bougares, Holger Schwenk, and Yoshua Bengio. 2014. Learning phrase representations using RNN encoder–decoder for statistical machine translation. In *Proc. of the 2014 Conference on Empirical Methods in Natural Language Processing (EMNLP)*, pages 1724–1734, Doha, Qatar. Association for Computational Linguistics. DOI: 10.3115/v1/d14-1179. 14

Kenneth Ward Church and Patrick Hanks. 1989. Word association norms, mutual information, and lexicography. In *27th Annual Meeting of the Association for Computational Linguistics*, pages 76–83, Vancouver, British Columbia, Canada. Association for Computational Linguistics. DOI: 10.3115/981623.981633. 1, 12, 19, 39, 40

Miruna-Adriana Clinciu and Helen Hastie. 2019. A survey of explainable AI terminology. In *Proc. of the 1st Workshop on Interactive Natural Language Technology for Explainable Artificial Intelligence (NL4XAI 2019)*, pages 8–13. Association for Computational Linguistics. DOI: 10.18653/v1/w19-8403.

Matthieu Courbariaux, Yoshua Bengio, and Jean-Pierre David. 2015. Binaryconnect: Training deep neural networks with binary weights during propagations. In *Advances in neural information processing systems*, pages 3123–3131. 26, 28

Matthieu Courbariaux, Itay Hubara, Daniel Soudry, Ran El-Yaniv, and Yoshua Bengio. 2016. Binarized neural networks: Training deep neural networks with weights and activations constrained to+ 1 or-1. *arXiv preprint arXiv:1602.02830.* 28

Róbert Csordás, Sjoerd van Steenkiste, and Jürgen Schmidhuber. 2021. Are neural nets modular? inspecting functional modularity through differentiable weight masks. In *International Conference on Learning Representations.* 28

Xiaoliang Dai, Hongxu Yin, and Niraj K. Jha. 2018. Grow and prune compact, fast, and accurate lstms. ArXiv 1805.11797. DOI: 10.1109/tc.2019.2954495. 36

Fahim Dalvi, Avery Nortonsmith, D. Anthony Bau, Yonatan Belinkov, Hassan Sajjad, Nadir Durrani, and James Glass. 2018. Neurox: A toolkit for analyzing individual neurons in neural networks. ArXiv 1812.09359. DOI: 10.1609/aaai.v33i01.33019851. 72

Marina Danilevsky, Kun Qian, Ranit Aharonov, Yannis Katsis, Ban Kawas, and Prithviraj Sen. 2020. A survey of the state of explainable AI for natural language processing. In *Proc. of the 1st Conference of the Asia-Pacific Chapter of the Association for Computational Linguistics and the 10th International Joint Conference on Natural Language Processing*, pages 447–459, Suzhou, China. Association for Computational Linguistics. 3, 4, 5, 9

Arun Das and Paul Rad. 2020. Opportunities and challenges in explainable artificial intelligence (xai): A survey. ArXiv 2006.11371. 4, 9, 10

Misha Denil, Alban Demiraj, Nal Kalchbrenner, Phil Blunsom, and Nando de Freitas. 2014. Modelling, visualising and summarising documents with a single convolutional neural network. *CoRR*, abs/1406.3830. 2, 5, 6, 12, 21

Joseph F. DeRose, Jiayao Wang, and Matthew Berger. 2020. Attention flows: Analyzing and comparing attention mechanisms in language models. ArXiv 2009.07053. DOI: 10.1109/tvcg.2020.3028976. 33

Jay DeYoung, Sarthak Jain, Nazneen Fatema Rajani, Eric Lehman, Caiming Xiong, Richard Socher, and Byron C. Wallace. 2020. ERASER: A benchmark to evaluate rationalized NLP models. In *Proc. of the 58th Annual Meeting of the Association for Computational Linguistics*, pages 4443–4458, Online. Association for Computational Linguistics. DOI: 10.18653/v1/2020.acl-main.408. 55, 61, 73

Amit Dhurandhar, Pin-Yu Chen, Ronny Luss, Chun-Chen Tu, Paishun Ting, Karthikeyan Shanmugam, and Payel Das. 2018. Explanations based on the missing: Towards contrastive explanations with pertinent negatives. ArXiv 1802.07623. 11, 65, 67, 71

Jürgen Dieber and Sabrina Kirrane. 2020. Why model why? assessing the strengths and limitations of lime. ArXiv 2012.00093. 51

Xiaohan Ding, guiguang ding, Xiangxin Zhou, Yuchen Guo, Jungong Han, and Ji Liu. 2019. Global sparse momentum sgd for pruning very deep neural networks. In *Advances in Neural Information Processing Systems*, volume 32. Curran Associates, Inc. 28

Yanzhuo Ding, Yang Liu, Huanbo Luan, and Maosong Sun. 2017. Visualizing and understanding neural machine translation. In *Proc. of the 55th Annual Meeting of the Association for Computational Linguistics (Volume 1: Long Papers)*, pages 1150–1159, Vancouver, Canada. Association for Computational Linguistics. DOI: 10.18653/v1/p17-1106. 22

Erik-Lân Do Dinh and Iryna Gurevych. 2016. Token-level metaphor detection using neural networks. In *Proc. of the Fourth Workshop on Metaphor in NLP*, pages 28–33, San Diego, California. Association for Computational Linguistics. DOI: 10.18653/v1/w16-1104. 28

Ann-Kathrin Dombrowski, Maximilian Alber, Christopher J. Anders, Marcel Ackermann, Klaus-Robert Müller, and Pan Kessel. 2019. Explanations can be manipulated and geometry is to blame. ArXiv 1906.07983. 58

Finale Doshi-Velez and Been Kim. 2017. Towards a rigorous science of interpretable machine learning. ArXiv 1702.08608. 55

Aleksandr Drozd, Anna Gladkova, and Satoshi Matsuoka. 2016. Word embeddings, analogies, and machine learning: Beyond king - man + woman = queen. In *Proc. of COLING 2016, the 26th International Conference on Computational Linguistics: Technical Papers*, pages 3519–3530, Osaka, Japan. The COLING 2016 Organizing Committee. 2, 40

Dheeru Dua, Yizhong Wang, Pradeep Dasigi, Gabriel Stanovsky, Sameer Singh, and Matt Gardner. 2019. DROP: A reading comprehension benchmark requiring discrete reasoning over paragraphs. In *Proc. of the 2019 Conference of the North American Chapter of the Association for Computational Linguistics: Human Language Technologies, Volume 1 (Long and Short Papers)*, pages 2368–2378, Minneapolis, Minnesota. Association for Computational Linguistics. DOI: 10.18653/v1/N19-1246. 50

Philipp Dufter and Hinrich Schütze. 2020. Identifying elements essential for BERT's multilinguality. In *Proc. of the 2020 Conference on Empirical Methods in Natural Language Processing (EMNLP)*, pages 4423–4437, Online. Association for Computational Linguistics. DOI: 10.18653/v1/2020.emnlp-main.358. 15

Yanai Elazar, Shauli Ravfogel, Alon Jacovi, and Yoav Goldberg. 2021. Amnesic probing: Behavioral explanation with amnesic counterfactuals. ArXiv 2006.00995. DOI: 10.1162/tacl_a_00359. 45

Radwa Elshawi, Mouaz Al-Mallah, and Sherif Sakr. 2019. On the interpretability of machine learning-based model for predicting hypertension. *BMC Med Inform Decis Mak.*, 19. DOI: 10.1186/s12911-019-0874-0. 50

Allyson Ettinger. 2020. What BERT is not: Lessons from a new suite of psycholinguistic diagnostics for language models. *Transactions of the Association for Computational Linguistics*, 8:34–48. DOI: 10.1162/tacl_a_00298. 19

Allyson Ettinger, Ahmed Elgohary, and Philip Resnik. 2016. Probing for semantic evidence of composition by means of simple classification tasks. In *Proc. of the 1st Workshop on Evaluating Vector-Space Representations for NLP*, pages 134–139, Berlin, Germany. Association for Computational Linguistics. DOI: 10.18653/v1/w16-2524. 44

Utku Evci, Yani Ioannou, Cem Keskin, and Yann Dauphin. 2021. Gradient flow in sparse neural networks and how lottery tickets win. ArXiv 2010.03533. 27

Stefan Evert. 2010. Distributional semantic models. In *NAACL HLT 2010 Tutorial Abstracts*, pages 15–18, Los Angeles, California. Association for Computational Linguistics. 39

Shi Feng and Jordan Boyd-Graber. 2019. What can ai do for me: Evaluating machine learning interpretations in cooperative play. ArXiv 1810.09648. DOI: 10.1145/3301275.3302265. 57, 61, 62

Ruth Fong, Mandela Patrick, and Andrea Vedaldi. 2019. Understanding deep networks via extremal perturbations and smooth masks. In *Proc. of the IEEE/CVF International Conference on Computer Vision (ICCV)*. DOI: 10.1109/iccv.2019.00304. 13

Ruth C. Fong and Andrea Vedaldi. 2017. Interpretable explanations of black boxes by meaningful perturbation. In *Proc. of the IEEE International Conference on Computer Vision (ICCV)*. DOI: 10.1109/iccv.2017.371. 72

James Forrest, Somayajulu Sripada, Wei Pang, and George Coghill. 2018. Towards making NLG a voice for interpretable machine learning. In *Proc. of the 11th International Conference on Natural Language Generation*, pages 177–182, Tilburg University, The Netherlands. Association for Computational Linguistics. DOI: 10.18653/v1/w18-6522. 56

Louis Fournier, Emmanuel Dupoux, and Ewan Dunbar. 2020. Analogies minus analogy test: measuring regularities in word embeddings. In *Proc. of the 24th Conference on Computational Natural Language Learning*, pages 365–375, Online. Association for Computational Linguistics. DOI: 10.18653/v1/2020.conll-1.29. 40

Jonathan Frankle and Michael Carbin. 2019. The lottery ticket hypothesis: Finding sparse, trainable neural networks. In *ICLR*. OpenReview.net. 18, 26

Jonathan Frankle, Gintare Karolina Dziugaite, Daniel M. Roy, and Michael Carbin. 2020. Stabilizing the lottery ticket hypothesis. ArXiv 1903.01611. 26

Alex Alves Freitas. 2013. Comprehensible classification models: a position paper. *SIGKDD Explor.*, 15(1):1–10. DOI: 10.1145/2594473.2594475. 25

Nicholas Frosst and Geoffrey Hinton. 2017. Distilling a neural network into a soft decision tree. ArXiv 1711.09784. 53

Jinlan Fu, Pengfei Liu, and Graham Neubig. 2020. Interpretable multi-dataset evaluation for named entity recognition. In *Proc. of the 2020 Conference on Empirical Methods in Natural Language Processing (EMNLP)*, pages 6058–6069, Online. Association for Computational Linguistics. DOI: 10.18653/v1/2020.emnlp-main.489. 54, 67, 73

Nicolas Garneau, Mareike Hartmann, Anders Sandholm, Sebastian Ruder, Ivan Vulic, and Anders Søgaard. 2021. Analogy training multilingual encoders. In *Proc. of the AAAI Conference on Artificial Intelligence*. 2, 12, 19, 40

Jon Gauthier and Roger Levy. 2019. Linking artificial and human neural representations of language. DOI: 10.18653/v1/d19-1050. 43

Reza Ghaeini, Xiaoli Fern, and Prasad Tadepalli. 2018. Interpreting recurrent and attention-based neural models: a case study on natural language inference. In *Proc. of the 2018 Conference on Empirical Methods in Natural Language Processing*, pages 4952–4957, Brussels, Belgium. Association for Computational Linguistics. DOI: 10.18653/v1/d18-1537. 31

Amirata Ghorbani, James Wexler, James Zou, and Been Kim. 2019. Towards automatic concept-based explanations. ArXiv 1902.03129. 46, 47, 71

Yoav Goldberg. 2017. *Neural Network Methods for Natural Language Processing*, volume 37 of *Synthesis Lectures on Human Language Technologies*. Morgan & Claypool, San Rafael, CA. DOI: 10.2200/S00762ED1V01Y201703HLT037. 15

Yoav Goldberg. 2019. Assessing bert's syntactic abilities. ArXiv 1901.05287. 49

Ana Valeria Gonzalez, Gagan Bansal, Angela Fan, Robin Jia, Yashar Mehdad, and Srinivasan Iyer. 2020. Human evaluation of spoken vs. visual explanations for open-domain qa. ArXiv 2012.15075. 62

Ana Valeria González, Maria Barrett, Rasmus Hvingelby, Kellie Webster, and Anders Søgaard. 2020. Type B reflexivization as an unambiguous testbed for multilingual multi-task gender bias. In *Proc. of the 2020 Conference on Empirical Methods in Natural Language Processing (EMNLP)*, pages 2637–2648, Online. Association for Computational Linguistics. DOI: 10.18653/v1/2020.emnlp-main.209. 50

Ana Valeria Gonzalez and Anders Søgaard. 2020. The reverse turing test for evaluating interpretability methods on unknown tasks. In *NeurIPS Workshop on Human And Machine in-the-Loop Evaluation and Learning Strategies*. 61, 62

Bryce Goodman and Seth Flaxman. 2017. European union regulations on algorithmic decision-making and a right to explanation. *AI Magazine*, 38(3):50–57. DOI: 10.1609/aimag.v38i3.2741. 68

Mitchell Gordon, Kevin Duh, and Nicholas Andrews. 2020. Compressing BERT: Studying the effects of weight pruning on transfer learning. In *Proc. of the 5th Workshop on Representation Learning for NLP*, pages 143–155, Online. Association for Computational Linguistics. DOI: 10.18653/v1/2020.repl4nlp-1.18. 26, 36

Yash Goyal, Amir Feder, Uri Shalit, and Been Kim. 2020. Explaining classifiers with causal concept effect (cace). ArXiv 1907.07165. 45

Sebastian Gruber. 2019. Lime and sampling. In Christoph Molnar, Ed., *Limitations of ML Interpretability*, chapter 13. Cristoph Molnar. 51

Riccardo Guidotti, Anna Monreale, Salvatore Ruggieri, Franco Turini, Fosca Giannotti, and Dino Pedreschi. 2018. A survey of methods for explaining black box models. *ACM Comput. Surv.*, 51(5). DOI: 10.1145/3236009. 3, 4, 6

Han Guo, Nazneen Fatema Rajani, Peter Hase, Mohit Bansal, and Caiming Xiong. 2020. Fastif: Scalable influence functions for efficient model interpretation and debugging. ArXiv 2012.15781. 51

Suchin Gururangan, Swabha Swayamdipta, Omer Levy, Roy Schwartz, Samuel Bowman, and Noah A. Smith. 2018. Annotation artifacts in natural language inference data. In *Proc. of the 2018 Conference of the North American Chapter of the Association for Computational Linguistics: Human Language Technologies, Volume 2 (Short Papers)*, pages 107–112, New Orleans, Louisiana. Association for Computational Linguistics. DOI: 10.18653/v1/n18-2017. 50

Song Han, Huizi Mao, and William J. Dally. 2015. Deep compression: Compressing deep neural networks with pruning, trained quantization and huffman coding. Cite arxiv:1510.00149Comment: Published as a conference paper at ICLR 2016 (oral). 25

Xiaochuang Han, Byron C. Wallace, and Yulia Tsvetkov. 2020. Explaining black box predictions and unveiling data artifacts through influence functions. In *Proc. of the 58th Annual Meeting of the Association for Computational Linguistics*, pages 5553–5563, Online. Association for Computational Linguistics. DOI: 10.18653/v1/2020.acl-main.492. 51

Kazuaki Hanawa, Sho Yokoi, Satoshi Hara, and Kentaro Inui. 2020. Evaluation criteria for instance-based explanation. ArXiv 2006.04528. 59

Yaru Hao, Li Dong, Furu Wei, and Ke Xu. 2021. Self-attention attribution: Interpreting information interactions inside transformer. ArXiv 2004.11207. 36, 37

Yiding Hao. 2020. Evaluating attribution methods using white-box lstms. ArXiv 2010.08606. DOI: 10.18653/v1/2020.blackboxnlp-1.28. 58

Mareike Hartmann and Anders Søgaard. 2018. Limitations of cross-lingual learning from image search. In *Proc. of The Third Workshop on Representation Learning for NLP*, pages 159–163, Melbourne, Australia. Association for Computational Linguistics. DOI: 10.18653/v1/w18-3021. 39

Peter Hase and Mohit Bansal. 2020. Evaluating explainable ai: Which algorithmic explanations help users predict model behavior? *arXiv preprint arXiv:2005.01831*. DOI: 10.18653/v1/2020.acl-main.491. 61, 62

John Hewitt and Percy Liang. 2019. Designing and interpreting probes with control tasks. In *Proc. of the 2019 Conference on Empirical Methods in Natural Language Processing and the 9th International Joint Conference on Natural Language Processing (EMNLP-IJCNLP)*, pages 2733–2743, Hong Kong, China. Association for Computational Linguistics. DOI: 10.18653/v1/d19-1275. 45

Kris Heylen, Dirk Speelman, and Dirk Geeraerts. 2012. Looking at word meaning. an interactive visualization of semantic vector spaces for Dutch synsets. In *Proc. of the EACL 2012 Joint Workshop of LINGVIS & UNCLH*, pages 16–24, Avignon, France. Association for Computational Linguistics. 12, 19

Avery Hiebert, Cole Peterson, Alona Fyshe, and Nishant Mehta. 2018. Interpreting word-level hidden state behaviour of character-level LSTM language models. In *Proc. of the 2018 EMNLP Workshop BlackboxNLP: Analyzing and Interpreting Neural Networks for NLP*, pages 258–266, Brussels, Belgium. Association for Computational Linguistics. DOI: 10.18653/v1/w18-5428. 44

Sepp Hochreiter and Jürgen Schmidhuber. 1997. Long short-term memory. *Neural computation*, 9(8):1735–1780. DOI: 10.1162/neco.1997.9.8.1735. 14

Nora Hollenstein, Antonio de la Torre, Nicolas Langer, and Ce Zhang. 2019. CogniVal: A framework for cognitive word embedding evaluation. In *Proc. of the 23rd Conference on Computational Natural Language Learning (CoNLL)*, pages 538–549, Hong Kong, China. Association for Computational Linguistics. DOI: 10.18653/v1/k19-1050. 43

Sara Hooker, Aaron Courville, Gregory Clark, Yann Dauphin, and Andrea Frome. 2020. What do compressed deep neural networks forget? ArXiv 1911.05248. 27

Benjamin Hoover, Hendrik Strobelt, and Sebastian Gehrmann. 2020. exBERT: A Visual Analysis Tool to Explore Learned Representations in Transformer Models. In *Proc. of the 58th Annual Meeting of the Association for Computational Linguistics: System Demonstrations*, pages 187–196, Online. Association for Computational Linguistics. DOI: 10.18653/v1/2020.acl-demos.22. 72

Bo-Jian Hou and Zhi-Hua Zhou. 2020. Learning with interpretable structure from gated rnn. ArXiv 1810.10708. DOI: 10.1109/tnnls.2020.2967051. 31

Phu Mon Htut, Jason Phang, Shikha Bordia, and Samuel R. Bowman. 2019. Do attention heads in bert track syntactic dependencies? ArXiv 1911.12246. 34

Jennifer Hu, Jon Gauthier, Peng Qian, Ethan Wilcox, and Roger P. Levy. 2020. A systematic assessment of syntactic generalization in neural language models. ArXiv 2005.03692. DOI: 10.18653/v1/2020.acl-main.158. 49

Zhiting Hu, Xuezhe Ma, Zhengzhong Liu, Eduard Hovy, and Eric Xing. 2016. Harnessing deep neural networks with logic rules. In *Proc. of the 54th Annual Meeting of the Association for Computational Linguistics (Volume 1: Long Papers)*, pages 2410–2420, Berlin, Germany. Association for Computational Linguistics. DOI: 10.18653/v1/p16-1228. 56

Itay Hubara, Matthieu Courbariaux, Daniel Soudry, Ran El-Yaniv, and Yoshua Bengio. 2016. Binarized neural networks. In *Advances in Neural Information Processing Systems*, volume 29. Curran Associates, Inc. 28

Alon Jacovi and Yoav Goldberg. 2020. Towards faithfully interpretable NLP systems: How should we define and evaluate faithfulness? In *Proc. of the 58th Annual Meeting of the Association for Computational Linguistics*, pages 4198–4205, Online. Association for Computational Linguistics. DOI: 10.18653/v1/2020.acl-main.386. 25, 58, 63, 67

Alon Jacovi and Yoav Goldberg. 2021. Aligning faithful interpretations with their social attribution. ArXiv 2006.01067. DOI: 10.1162/tacl_a_00367. 55

Sarthak Jain and Byron C. Wallace. 2019. Attention is not Explanation. In *Proc. of the 2019 Conference of the North American Chapter of the Association for Computational Linguistics: Human Language Technologies, Volume 1 (Long and Short Papers)*, pages 3543–3556, Minneapolis, Minnesota. Association for Computational Linguistics. 32

Joseph D. Janizek, Pascal Sturmfels, and Su-In Lee. 2020. Explaining explanations: Axiomatic feature interactions for deep networks. ArXiv 2002.04138. 72

Ganesh Jawahar, Benoît Sagot, and Djamé Seddah. 2019. What does BERT learn about the structure of language? In *Proc. of the 57th Annual Meeting of the Association for Computational Linguistics*, pages 3651–3657, Florence, Italy. Association for Computational Linguistics. DOI: 10.18653/v1/p19-1356. 44

Serena Jeblee, Mireille Gomes, and Graeme Hirst. 2018. Multi-task learning for interpretable cause of death classification using key phrase prediction. In *Proc. of the BioNLP 2018 workshop*, pages 12–17, Melbourne, Australia. Association for Computational Linguistics. DOI: 10.18653/v1/w18-2302. 56

Anupama Jha, Joseph K. Aicher, Deependra Singh, and Yoseph Barash. 2019. Improving interpretability of deep learning models: splicing codes as a case study. *bioRxiv*. DOI: 10.1101/700096. 23

Jae-young Jo and Sung-Hyon Myaeng. 2020. Roles and utilization of attention heads in transformer-based neural language models. In *Proc. of the 58th Annual Meeting of the Association for Computational Linguistics*, pages 3404–3417, Online. Association for Computational Linguistics. DOI: 10.18653/v1/2020.acl-main.311. 72

Ákos Kádár, Grzegorz Chrupała, and Afra Alishahi. 2017. Representation of linguistic form and function in recurrent neural networks. *Computational Linguistics*, 43(4):761–780. DOI: 10.1162/coli_a_00300. 41

Yova Kementchedjhieva and Adam Lopez. 2018. 'indicatements' that character language models learn English morpho-syntactic units and regularities. In *Proc. of the 2018 EMNLP Workshop BlackboxNLP: Analyzing and Interpreting Neural Networks for NLP*, pages 145–153, Brussels, Belgium. Association for Computational Linguistics. DOI: 10.18653/v1/w18-5417. 26

Urvashi Khandelwal, Omer Levy, Dan Jurafsky, Luke Zettlemoyer, and Mike Lewis. 2020. Generalization through memorization: Nearest neighbor language models. In *International Conference on Learning Representations*. 16

Been Kim, Martin Wattenberg, Justin Gilmer, Carrie Cai, James Wexler, Fernanda Viegas, and Rory Sayres. 2018. Interpretability beyond feature attribution: Quantitative testing with concept activation vectors (tcav). ArXiv 1711.11279. 3, 5, 12, 19, 44, 45, 46, 72

Siwon Kim, Jihun Yi, Eunji Kim, and Sungroh Yoon. 2020. Interpretation of NLP models through input marginalization. In *Proc. of the 2020 Conference on Empirical Methods in Natural Language Processing (EMNLP)*, pages 3154–3167, Online. Association for Computational Linguistics. DOI: 10.18653/v1/2020.emnlp-main.255. 24

Yoon Kim and Alexander M. Rush. 2016. Sequence-level knowledge distillation. In *Proc. of the 2016 Conference on Empirical Methods in Natural Language Processing*, pages 1317–1327, Austin, Texas. Association for Computational Linguistics. DOI: 10.18653/v1/d16-1139. 12, 20, 53

Young Jin Kim and Hany Hassan. 2020. FastFormers: Highly efficient transformer models for natural language understanding. In *Proc. of SustaiNLP: Workshop on Simple and Efficient Nat-*

ural Language Processing, pages 149–158, Online. Association for Computational Linguistics. DOI: 10.18653/v1/2020.sustainlp-1.20. 25

Pieter-Jan Kindermans, Sara Hooker, Julius Adebayo, Maximilian Alber, Kristof T. Schütt, Sven Dähne, Dumitru Erhan, and Been Kim. 2017. The (un)reliability of saliency methods. DOI: 10.1007/978-3-030-28954-6_14. 58, 61

Pieter-Jan Kindermans, Kristof Schütt, Klaus-Robert Müller, and Sven Dähne. 2016. Investigating the influence of noise and distractors on the interpretation of neural networks. ArXiv 1611.07270. 22

Goro Kobayashi, Tatsuki Kuribayashi, Sho Yokoi, and Kentaro Inui. 2020. Attention is not only a weight: Analyzing transformers with vector norms. In *Proc. of the 2020 Conference on Empirical Methods in Natural Language Processing (EMNLP)*, pages 7057–7075, Online. Association for Computational Linguistics. DOI: 10.18653/v1/2020.emnlp-main.574. 12, 18, 32

Konstantin Kobs, Tobias Koopmann, Albin Zehe, David Fernes, Philipp Krop, and Andreas Hotho. 2020. Where to submit? helping researchers to choose the right venue. In *Findings of the Association for Computational Linguistics: EMNLP 2020*, pages 878–883, Online. Association for Computational Linguistics. DOI: 10.18653/v1/2020.findings-emnlp.78. 23

Pang Wei Koh and Percy Liang. 2017. Understanding black-box predictions via influence functions. In *Proc. of the 34th International Conference on Machine Learning*, volume 70 of *Proc. of Machine Learning Research*, pages 1885–1894, International Convention Centre, Sydney, Australia. PMLR. 5, 12, 20, 46, 50, 51

Pang Wei Koh, Thao Nguyen, Yew Siang Tang, Stephen Mussmann, Emma Pierson, Been Kim, and Percy Liang. 2020. Concept bottleneck models. ArXiv 2007.04612. 46

Narine Kokhlikyan, Vivek Miglani, Miguel Martin, Edward Wang, Bilal Alsallakh, Jonathan Reynolds, Alexander Melnikov, Natalia Kliushkina, Carlos Araya, Siqi Yan, and Orion Reblitz-Richardson. 2020. Captum: A unified and generic model interpretability library for pytorch. ArXiv 2009.07896. 71

Prasanth Kolachina, Nicola Cancedda, Marc Dymetman, and Sriram Venkatapathy. 2012. Prediction of learning curves in machine translation. In *Proc. of the 50th Annual Meeting of the Association for Computational Linguistics (Volume 1: Long Papers)*, pages 22–30, Jeju Island, Korea. Association for Computational Linguistics. 54

Philipp Kopper. 2019. Lime and neighborhood. In Christoph Molnar, Ed., *Limitations of ML Interpretability*, chapter 13. Christoph Molnar. 51

Neema Kotonya and Francesca Toni. 2020. Explainable automated fact-checking: A survey. In *Proc. of the 28th International Conference on Computational Linguistics*, pages 5430–5443, Barcelona, Spain (Online). International Committee on Computational Linguistics. 3, 10

Nikolaus Kriegeskorte, Marieke Mur, and Peter Bandettini. 2008. Representational similarity analysis–connecting the branches of systems neuroscience. *Frontiers in Systems Neuroscience*, 3. DOI: 10.3389/neuro.06.004.2008. 5, 19, 43

Sandra Kubler, Ryan McDonald, Joakim Nivre, and Graeme Hirst. 2009. *Dependency Parsing*. Morgan & Claypool. DOI: 10.2200/S00169ED1V01Y200901HLT002. 16

Jenny Kunz and Marco Kuhlmann. 2020. Classifier probes may just learn from linear context features. In *Proc. of the 28th International Conference on Computational Linguistics*, pages 5136–5146, Barcelona, Spain (Online). International Committee on Computational Linguistics. DOI: 10.18653/v1/2020.coling-main.450. 44

Isaac Lage, Emily Chen, Jeffrey He, Menaka Narayanan, Been Kim, Sam Gershman, and Finale Doshi-Velez. 2019. An evaluation of the human-interpretability of explanation. ArXiv 1902.00006. 25

Vivian Lai and Chenhao Tan. 2019. On human predictions with explanations and predictions of machine learning models. *Proc. of the Conference on Fairness, Accountability, and Transparency*. DOI: 10.1145/3287560.3287590. 56

Yair Lakretz, German Kruszewski, Theo Desbordes, Dieuwke Hupkes, Stanislas Dehaene, and Marco Baroni. 2019. The emergence of number and syntax units in LSTM language models. In *Proc. of the 2019 Conference of the North American Chapter of the Association for Computational Linguistics: Human Language Technologies, Volume 1 (Long and Short Papers)*, pages 11–20, Minneapolis, Minnesota. Association for Computational Linguistics. 12, 15, 18, 26, 31

Matthew Lamm, Jennimaria Palomaki, Chris Alberti, Daniel Andor, Eunsol Choi, Livio Baldini Soares, and Michael Collins. 2020. Qed: A framework and dataset for explanations in question answering. ArXiv 2009.06354. 61, 62, 73

Xu Lan, Xiatian Zhu, and Shaogang Gong. 2018. Knowledge distillation by on-the-fly native ensemble. In *Advances in Neural Information Processing Systems*, volume 31. Curran Associates, Inc. 53

Sebastian Lapuschkin, Alexander Binder, Grégoire Montavon, Klaus-Robert Müller, and Wojciech Samek. 2016. The lrp toolbox for artificial neural networks. *Journal of Machine Learning Research*, 17(114):1–5. 72

Thibault Laugel, Xavier Renard, Marie-Jeanne Lesot, Christophe Marsala, and Marcin Detyniecki. 2018. Defining locality for surrogates in post-hoc interpretablity. *arXiv preprint arXiv:1806.07498*. 51

Anne Lauscher, Vinit Ravishankar, Ivan Vulić, and Goran Glavaš. 2020. From zero to hero: On the limitations of zero-shot language transfer with multilingual Transformers. In *Proc. of the 2020 Conference on Empirical Methods in Natural Language Processing (EMNLP)*, pages 4483–4499, Online. Association for Computational Linguistics. DOI: 10.18653/v1/2020.emnlp-main.363. 54

Erwan Le Merrer and Gilles Trédan. 2020. Remote explainability faces the bouncer problem. *Nature Machine Intelligence*, 2(9):529–539. DOI: 10.1038/s42256-020-0216-z. 63

Yann LeCun, John Denker, and Sara Solla. 1990. Optimal brain damage. In *Advances in Neural Information Processing Systems*, volume 2. Morgan-Kaufmann. 25

Gyeongbok Lee, Seung-won Hwang, and Hyunsouk Cho. 2020. SQuAD2-CR: Semi-supervised annotation for cause and rationales for unanswerability in SQuAD 2.0. In *Proc. of the 12th Language Resources and Evaluation Conference*, pages 5425–5432, Marseille, France. European Language Resources Association. 61

Tao Lei, Regina Barzilay, and Tommi Jaakkola. 2016. Rationalizing neural predictions. In *Proc. of the 2016 Conference on Empirical Methods in Natural Language Processing*, pages 107–117, Austin, Texas. Association for Computational Linguistics. DOI: 10.18653/v1/d16-1011. 56

Philippe Leray, Patrick Gallinari, Patrick Gallinari, and Patrick Gallinari. 1998. Feature selection with neural networks. *Behaviormetrika*, 26:16–6. DOI: 10.2333/bhmk.26.145. 5, 6, 12, 21

Jiawei Li, Yiming Li, Xingchun Xiang, Shu-Tao Xia, Siyi Dong, and Yun Cai. 2020. Tnt: An interpretable tree-network-tree learning framework using knowledge distillation. *Entropy*, 22(11). DOI: 10.3390/e22111203. 53

Wang Ling, Dani Yogatama, Chris Dyer, and Phil Blunsom. 2017. Program induction by rationale generation: Learning to solve and explain algebraic word problems. In *Proc. of the 55th Annual Meeting of the Association for Computational Linguistics (Volume 1: Long Papers)*, pages 158–167, Vancouver, Canada. Association for Computational Linguistics. DOI: 10.18653/v1/p17-1015. 73

Junjie Liu, Zhe Xu, Runbin Shi, Ray C. C. Cheung, and Hayden K. H. So. 2020. Dynamic sparse training: Find efficient sparse network from scratch with trainable masked layers. In *International Conference on Learning Representations*. 25

Nelson F. Liu, Roy Schwartz, and Noah A. Smith. 2019. Inoculation by fine-tuning: A method for analyzing challenge datasets. In *Proc. of the 2019 Conference of the North American Chapter of the Association for Computational Linguistics: Human Language Technologies, Volume 1 (Long and Short Papers)*, pages 2171–2179, Minneapolis, Minnesota. Association for Computational Linguistics. DOI: 10.18653/v1/n19-1225. 5, 12, 19

Xuan Liu, Di Cao, and Kai Yu. 2018. Binarized LSTM language model. In *Proc. of the 2018 Conference of the North American Chapter of the Association for Computational Linguistics: Human Language Technologies, Volume 1 (Long Papers)*, pages 2113–2121, New Orleans, Louisiana. Association for Computational Linguistics. DOI: 10.18653/v1/n18-1192. 29

Zihan Liu, Genta Indra Winata, Samuel Cahyawijaya, Andrea Madotto, Zhaojiang Lin, and Pascale Fung. 2020. On the importance of word order information in cross-lingual sequence labeling. ArXiv 2001.11164. 15

Kaiji Lu, Piotr Mardziel, Klas Leino, Matt Fredrikson, and Anupam Datta. 2020. Influence paths for characterizing subject-verb number agreement in LSTM language models. In *Proc. of the 58th Annual Meeting of the Association for Computational Linguistics*, pages 4748–4757, Online. Association for Computational Linguistics. DOI: 10.18653/v1/2020.acl-main.430. 23

Scott Lundberg and Su-In Lee. 2017. A unified approach to interpreting model predictions. ArXiv 1705.07874. 64

Eran Malach, Gilad Yehudai, Shai Shalev-Schwartz, and Ohad Shamir. 2020. Proving the lottery ticket hypothesis: Pruning is all you need. In *Proc. of the 37th International Conference on Machine Learning*, volume 119 of *Proc. of Machine Learning Research*, pages 6682–6691. PMLR. 27

Yihuan Mao, Yujing Wang, Chufan Wu, Chen Zhang, Yang Wang, Quanlu Zhang, Yaming Yang, Yunhai Tong, and Jing Bai. 2020. LadaBERT: Lightweight adaptation of BERT through hybrid model compression. In *Proc. of the 28th International Conference on Computational Linguistics*, pages 3225–3234, Barcelona, Spain (Online). International Committee on Computational Linguistics. DOI: 10.18653/v1/2020.coling-main.287. 26

Ana Marasović, Chandra Bhagavatula, Jae sung Park, Ronan Le Bras, Noah A. Smith, and Yejin Choi. 2020. Natural language rationales with full-stack visual reasoning: From pixels to semantic frames to commonsense graphs. In *Findings of the Association for Computational Linguistics: EMNLP 2020*, pages 2810–2829, Online. Association for Computational Linguistics. DOI: 10.18653/v1/2020.findings-emnlp.253. 56, 59

André F. T. Martins, António Farinhas, Marcos Treviso, Vlad Niculae, Pedro M. Q. Aguiar, and Mário A. T. Figueiredo. 2020. Sparse and continuous attention mechanisms. ArXiv 2006.07214. 28

R. Thomas McCoy, Ellie Pavlick, and Tal Linzen. 2019. Right for the wrong reasons: Diagnosing syntactic heuristics in natural language inference. ArXiv 1902.01007. DOI: 10.18653/v1/p19-1334. 49

Ryan McDonald, Fernando Pereira, Kiril Ribarov, and Jan Hajič. 2005. Non-projective dependency parsing using spanning tree algorithms. In *Proc. of Human Language Technology Conference and Conference on Empirical Methods in Natural Language Processing*, pages 523–530, Vancouver, British Columbia, Canada. Association for Computational Linguistics. DOI: 10.3115/1220575.1220641. 34

Paul Michel, Omer Levy, and Graham Neubig. 2019. Are sixteen heads really better than one? ArXiv 1905.10650. 36, 37

Tomas Mikolov, Kai Chen, Greg Corrado, and Jeffrey Dean. 2013a. Distributed representations of words and phrases and their compositionality. In *Proc. of the 27th Annual Conference on Neural Information Processing Systems*, pages 3111–3119. 2, 12, 19, 40, 43, 44

Tomas Mikolov, Quoc V. Le, and Ilya Sutskever. 2013b. Exploiting similarities among languages for machine translation. ArXiv 1309.4168. 5

Ishan Misra, Abhinav Shrivastava, Abhinav Gupta, and Martial Hebert. 2016. Cross-stitch networks for multi-task learning. ArXiv 1604.03539. DOI: 10.1109/cvpr.2016.433. 26, 27

Brent Daniel Mittelstadt, Patrick Allo, Mariarosaria Taddeo, Sandra Wachter, and Luciano Floridi. 2016. The ethics of algorithms: Mapping the debate. *Big Data & Society*, 3(2). DOI: 10.1177/2053951716679679. 68

Akash Kumar Mohankumar, Preksha Nema, Sharan Narasimhan, Mitesh M. Khapra, Balaji Vasan Srinivasan, and Balaraman Ravindran. 2020. Towards transparent and explainable attention models. In *Proc. of the 58th Annual Meeting of the Association for Computational Linguistics*, pages 4206–4216, Online. Association for Computational Linguistics. DOI: 10.18653/v1/2020.acl-main.387. 32

Pavlo Molchanov, Arun Mallya, Stephen Tyree, Iuri Frosio, and Jan Kautz. 2019. Importance estimation for neural network pruning. In *IEEE Conference on Computer Vision and Pattern Recognition, CVPR 2019, Long Beach, CA, June 16-20, 2019*, pages 11264–11272. Computer Vision Foundation / IEEE. DOI: 10.1109/cvpr.2019.01152. 25

Christoph Molnar. 2019. *Interpretable Machine Learning*. https://christophm.github.io/interpretable-ml-book/ DOI: 10.1007/978-3-030-65965-3_28. 3, 4, 8, 11

Grégoire Montavon, Sebastian Lapuschkin, Alexander Binder, Wojciech Samek, and Klaus-Robert Müller. 2017. Explaining nonlinear classification decisions with deep taylor decomposition. *Pattern Recognition*, 65:211–222. DOI: 10.1016/j.patcog.2016.11.008. 5, 7, 12, 17, 22, 23, 65

Pooya Moradi, Nishant Kambhatla, and Anoop Sarkar. 2019. Interrogating the explanatory power of attention in neural machine translation. In *Proc. of the 3rd Workshop on Neural Generation and Translation*, pages 221–230, Hong Kong. Association for Computational Linguistics. DOI: 10.18653/v1/d19-5624. 32

Raha Moraffah, Mansooreh Karami, Ruocheng Guo, Adrienne Raglin, and Huan Liu. 2020. Causal interpretability for machine learning–problems, methods and evaluation. ArXiv 2003.03934. DOI: 10.1145/3400051.3400058. 46

Ari S. Morcos, Haonan Yu, Michela Paganini, and Yuandong Tian. 2019. One ticket to win them all: generalizing lottery ticket initializations across datasets and optimizers. ArXiv 1906.02773. 26

Ramaravind K. Mothilal, Amit Sharma, and Chenhao Tan. 2020. Explaining machine learning classifiers through diverse counterfactual explanations. *Proc. of the 2020 Conference on Fairness, Accountability, and Transparency*. DOI: 10.1145/3351095.3372850. 67, 71

Rajiv Movva and Jason Zhao. 2020. Dissecting lottery ticket transformers: Structural and behavioral study of sparse neural machine translation. In *Proc. of the Third BlackboxNLP Workshop on Analyzing and Interpreting Neural Networks for NLP*, pages 193–203, Online. Association for Computational Linguistics. DOI: 10.18653/v1/2020.blackboxnlp-1.19. 18, 27

Pramod Kaushik Mudrakarta, Ankur Taly, Mukund Sundararajan, and Kedar Dhamdhere. 2018. Did the model understand the question? In *Proc. of the 56th Annual Meeting of the Association for Computational Linguistics (Volume 1: Long Papers)*, pages 1896–1906, Melbourne, Australia. Association for Computational Linguistics. DOI: 10.18653/v1/p18-1176. 5, 7, 12, 17, 23, 65

James Mullenbach, Jonathan Gordon, Nanyun Peng, and Jonathan May. 2019. Do nuclear submarines have nuclear captains? a challenge dataset for commonsense reasoning over adjectives and objects. In *Proc. of the 2019 Conference on Empirical Methods in Natural Language Processing and the 9th International Joint Conference on Natural Language Processing (EMNLP-IJCNLP)*, pages 6052–6058, Hong Kong, China. Association for Computational Linguistics. DOI: 10.18653/v1/d19-1625. 5, 12, 19

W. James Murdoch, Peter J. Liu, and Bin Yu. 2018. Beyond word importance: Contextual decomposition to extract interactions from LSTMs. In *International Conference on Learning Representations*. 40, 56, 60

Brian Murphy, Partha Talukdar, and Tom Mitchell. 2012. Learning effective and interpretable semantic models using non-negative sparse embedding. In *Proc. of COLING 2012*, pages 1933–1950, Mumbai, India. The COLING 2012 Organizing Committee. 29

Aakanksha Naik, Abhilasha Ravichander, Norman Sadeh, Carolyn Rose, and Graham Neubig. 2018. Stress test evaluation for natural language inference. In *Proc. of the 27th International Conference on Computational Linguistics*, pages 2340–2353, Santa Fe, New Mexico, Association for Computational Linguistics. 50

Sharan Narang, Colin Raffel, Katherine Lee, Adam Roberts, Noah Fiedel, and Karishma Malkan. 2020. Wt5?! training text-to-text models to explain their predictions. 20, 59

Dong Nguyen. 2018. Comparing automatic and human evaluation of local explanations for text classification. In *Proc. of the 2018 Conference of the North American Chapter of the Association for Computational Linguistics: Human Language Technologies, Volume 1 (Long Papers)*, pages 1069–1078, New Orleans, Louisiana. Association for Computational Linguistics. DOI: 10.18653/v1/n18-1097. 61

Richard Nisbett and Timothy DeCamp Wilson. 1977. Telling more than we can know: Verbal reports on mental processes. *Psychological Review*, 84(3). DOI: 10.1037/0033-295x.84.3.231. 57

Christopher Olah, Arvind Satyanarayan, Ian Johnson, Shan Carter, Ludwig Schubert, Katherine Ye, and Alexander Mordvintsev. 2018. The building blocks of interpretability. *Distill*. DOI: 10.23915/distill.00010. 67

B. A. Olshausen and D. J. Field. 1996. Emergence of simple-cell receptive field properties by learning a sparse code for natural images. *Nature*, 381:607–609. DOI: 10.1038/381607a0. 26, 29

Laurent Orseau, Marcus Hutter, and Omar Rivasplata. 2020. Logarithmic pruning is all you need. ArXiv 2006.12156. 27

Michela Paganini. 2020. Prune responsibly. ArXiv 2009.09936. 27

Bhargavi Paranjape, Mandar Joshi, John Thickstun, Hannaneh Hajishirzi, and Luke Zettlemoyer. 2020. An information bottleneck approach for controlling conciseness in rationale extraction. In *Proc. of the 2020 Conference on Empirical Methods in Natural Language Processing (EMNLP)*, pages 1938–1952, Online. Association for Computational Linguistics. DOI: 10.18653/v1/2020.emnlp-main.153. 28

Slav Petrov, Pi-Chuan Chang, Michael Ringgaard, and Hiyan Alshawi. 2010. Uptraining for accurate deterministic question parsing. In *Proc. of the 2010 Conference on Empirical Methods in Natural Language Processing*, pages 705–713, Cambridge, MA. Association for Computational Linguistics. 5, 12, 20, 50, 53, 54

Tiago Pimentel, Josef Valvoda, Rowan Hall Maudslay, Ran Zmigrod, Adina Williams, and Ryan Cotterell. 2020. Information-theoretic probing for linguistic structure. In *Proc. of the*

58th Annual Meeting of the Association for Computational Linguistics, pages 4609–4622, Online. Association for Computational Linguistics. DOI: 10.18653/v1/2020.acl-main.420. 45

Nina Poerner, Hinrich Schütze, and Benjamin Roth. 2018. Evaluating neural network explanation methods using hybrid documents and morphosyntactic agreement. In *Proc. of the 56th Annual Meeting of the Association for Computational Linguistics (Volume 1: Long Papers)*, pages 340–350, Melbourne, Australia. Association for Computational Linguistics. DOI: 10.18653/v1/p18-1032. 22, 24, 51

Sai Prasanna, Anna Rogers, and Anna Rumshisky. 2020. When BERT Plays the Lottery, All Tickets Are Winning. In *Proc. of the 2020 Conference on Empirical Methods in Natural Language Processing (EMNLP)*, pages 3208–3229, Online. Association for Computational Linguistics. DOI: 10.18653/v1/2020.emnlp-main.259. 27

Nicolas Pröllochs, Stefan Feuerriegel, and Dirk Neumann. 2019. Learning interpretable negation rules via weak supervision at document level: A reinforcement learning approach. In *Proc. of the 2019 Conference of the North American Chapter of the Association for Computational Linguistics: Human Language Technologies, Volume 1 (Long and Short Papers)*, pages 407–413, Minneapolis, Minnesota. Association for Computational Linguistics. DOI: 10.18653/v1/n19-1038. 9

Danish Pruthi, Mansi Gupta, Bhuwan Dhingra, Graham Neubig, and Zachary C. Lipton. 2020a. Learning to deceive with attention-based explanations. In *Proc. of the 58th Annual Meeting of the Association for Computational Linguistics*, pages 4782–4793, Online. Association for Computational Linguistics. DOI: 10.18653/v1/2020.acl-main.432. 5, 6, 32

Garima Pruthi, Frederick Liu, Mukund Sundararajan, and Satyen Kale. 2020b. Estimating training data influence by tracing gradient descent. ArXiv 2002.08484. 46

Alec Radford, Rafal Jozefowicz, and Ilya Sutskever. 2017. Learning to generate reviews and discovering sentiment. ArXiv 1704.01444. 26

Alessandro Raganato and Jörg Tiedemann. 2018. An analysis of encoder representations in transformer-based machine translation. In *Proc. of the 2018 EMNLP Workshop BlackboxNLP: Analyzing and Interpreting Neural Networks for NLP*, pages 287–297, Brussels, Belgium. Association for Computational Linguistics. DOI: 10.18653/v1/w18-5431. 32, 34

Ramchalam Kinattinkara Ramakrishnan, Eyyüb Sari, and Vahid Partovi Nia. 2020. Differentiable mask for pruning convolutional and recurrent networks. DOI: 10.1109/crv50864.2020.00037. 28

Karthikeyan Natesan Ramamurthy, Bhanukiran Vinzamuri, Yunfeng Zhang, and Amit Dhurandhar. 2020. Model agnostic multilevel explanations. ArXiv 2003.06005. 3, 67

Sahana Ramnath, Preksha Nema, Deep Sahni, and Mitesh M. Khapra. 2020. Towards interpreting BERT for reading comprehension based QA. In *Proc. of the 2020 Conference on Empirical Methods in Natural Language Processing (EMNLP)*, pages 3236–3242, Online. Association for Computational Linguistics. DOI: 10.18653/v1/2020.emnlp-main.261. 23

Abhilasha Ravichander, Aakanksha Naik, Carolyn Rose, and Eduard Hovy. 2019. EQUATE: A benchmark evaluation framework for quantitative reasoning in natural language inference. In *Proc. of the 23rd Conference on Computational Natural Language Learning (CoNLL)*, pages 349–361, Hong Kong, China. Association for Computational Linguistics. DOI: 10.18653/v1/k19-1033. 73

Vinit Ravishankar, Memduh Gökırmak, Lilja Øvrelid, and Erik Velldal. 2019. Multilingual probing of deep pre-trained contextual encoders. In *Proc. of the First NLPL Workshop on Deep Learning for Natural Language Processing*, pages 37–47, Turku, Finland. Linköping University Electronic Press. 44

Vinit Ravishankar, Artur Kulmizev, Mostafa Abdou, Anders Søgaard, and Joakim Nivre. 2021. Attention can reflect syntactic structure (if you let it). ArXiv 2101.10927. 12, 18, 34, 66

Marek Rei and Anders Søgaard. 2018. Zero-shot sequence labeling: Transferring knowledge from sentences to tokens. In *Proc. of the 2018 Conference of the North American Chapter of the Association for Computational Linguistics: Human Language Technologies, Volume 1 (Long Papers)*, pages 293–302, New Orleans, Louisiana. Association for Computational Linguistics. DOI: 10.18653/v1/n18-1027. 3, 5, 12, 18, 31, 56, 60, 73

Emily Reif, Ann Yuan, Martin Wattenberg, Fernanda B. Viegas, Andy Coenen, Adam Pearce, and Been Kim. 2019. Visualizing and measuring the geometry of bert. In *Advances in Neural Information Processing Systems*, volume 32. Curran Associates, Inc. 12, 19

Ehud Reiter. 2019. Natural language generation challenges for explainable AI. In *Proc. of the 1st Workshop on Interactive Natural Language Technology for Explainable Artificial Intelligence (NL4XAI 2019)*, pages 3–7. Association for Computational Linguistics. DOI: 10.18653/v1/w19-8402. 56, 57

Alex Renda, Jonathan Frankle, and Michael Carbin. 2020. Comparing rewinding and fine-tuning in neural network pruning. ArXiv 2003.02389. 27

Marco Tulio Ribeiro, Sameer Singh, and Carlos Guestrin. 2016. why should i trust you? explaining the predictions of any classifier. In *Proc. of the 22nd ACM SIGKDD international conference on knowledge discovery and data mining*, pages 1135–1144. DOI: 10.1145/2939672.2939778. 4, 5, 8, 10, 12, 20, 50, 61, 63, 64, 65, 71

Marco Tulio Ribeiro, Sameer Singh, and Carlos Guestrin. 2018. Semantically equivalent adversarial rules for debugging NLP models. In *Proc. of the 56th Annual Meeting of the Association for Computational Linguistics (Volume 1: Long Papers)*, pages 856–865, Melbourne, Australia. Association for Computational Linguistics. DOI: 10.18653/v1/p18-1079. 3, 67

Marco Tulio Ribeiro, Tongshuang Wu, Carlos Guestrin, and Sameer Singh. 2020. Beyond accuracy: Behavioral testing of NLP models with CheckList. In *Proc. of the 58th Annual Meeting of the Association for Computational Linguistics*, pages 4902–4912, Online. Association for Computational Linguistics. DOI: 10.18653/v1/2020.acl-main.442. 50

Matthew Richardson, Christopher J. C. Burges, and Erin Renshaw. 2013. MCTest: A challenge dataset for the open-domain machine comprehension of text. In *Proc. of the 2013 Conference on Empirical Methods in Natural Language Processing*, pages 193–203, Seattle, Washington, Association for Computational Linguistics. 5, 12, 19

Marc Riera, José-María Arnau, and Antonio González. 2019. CGPA: coarse-grained pruning of activations for energy-efficient RNN inference. *IEEE Micro*, 39(5):36–45. DOI: 10.1109/mm.2019.2929742. 36

Anna Rogers, Aleksandr Drozd, and Bofang Li. 2017. The (too many) problems of analogical reasoning with word vectors. In *Proc. of the 6th Joint Conference on Lexical and Computational Semantics (*SEM 2017)*, pages 135–148, Vancouver, Canada. Association for Computational Linguistics. DOI: 10.18653/v1/s17-1017. 40

Anna Rogers, Olga Kovaleva, and Anna Rumshisky. 2020. A primer in BERTology: What we know about how BERT works. *Transactions of the Association for Computational Linguistics*, 8:842–866. DOI: 10.1162/tacl_a_00349. 49

Sebastian Ruder, Joachim Bingel, Isabelle Augenstein, and Anders Søgaard. 2018. Latent multi-task architecture learning. ArXiv 1705.08142. DOI: 10.1609/aaai.v33i01.33014822. 27, 28

Tatyana Ruzsics, Olga Sozinova, Ximena Gutierrez-Vasques, and Tanja Samardzic. 2021. Interpretability for morphological inflection: from character-level predictions to subword-level rules. In *Proc. of the 16th Conference of the European Chapter of the Association for Computational Linguistics: Main Volume*, pages 3189–3201, Online. Association for Computational Linguistics. 10

Wojciech Samek, Grégoire Montavon, Sebastian Lapuschkin, Christopher J. Anders, and Klaus-Robert Müller. 2021. Explaining deep neural networks and beyond: A review of methods and applications. *Proc. of the IEEE*, 109(3):247–278. DOI: 10.1109/jproc.2021.3060483. 65

Maarten Sap, Ronan Le Bras, Emily Allaway, Chandra Bhagavatula, Nicholas Lourie, Hannah Rashkin, Brendan Roof, Noah A. Smith, and Yejin Choi. 2019. Atomic: An atlas of machine commonsense for if-then reasoning. ArXiv 1811.00146. DOI: 10.1609/aaai.v33i01.33013027. 73

Naomi Saphra and Adam Lopez. 2020. LSTMs compose—and Learn—Bottom-up. In *Findings of the Association for Computational Linguistics: EMNLP 2020*, pages 2797–2809, Online. Association for Computational Linguistics. DOI: 10.18653/v1/2020.findings-emnlp.252. 41

Marten van Schijndel, Aaron Mueller, and Tal Linzen. 2019. Quantity doesn't buy quality syntax with neural language models. In *Proc. of the 2019 Conference on Empirical Methods in Natural Language Processing and the 9th International Joint Conference on Natural Language Processing (EMNLP-IJCNLP)*, pages 5831–5837, Hong Kong, China. Association for Computational Linguistics. DOI: 10.18653/v1/d19-1592. 49

Robert Schwarzenberg, Marc Hübner, David Harbecke, Christoph Alt, and Leonhard Hennig. 2019a. Layerwise relevance visualization in convolutional text graph classifiers. In *Proc. of the Thirteenth Workshop on Graph-Based Methods for Natural Language Processing (TextGraphs-13)*, pages 58–62, Hong Kong. Association for Computational Linguistics. DOI: 10.18653/v1/d19-5308. 23

Robert Schwarzenberg, Lisa Raithel, and David Harbecke. 2019b. Neural vector conceptualization for word vector space interpretation. In *Proc. of the 3rd Workshop on Evaluating Vector Space Representations for NLP*, pages 1–7, Minneapolis, Association for Computational Linguistics. DOI: 10.18653/v1/w19-2001. 46

Abigail See, Minh-Thang Luong, and Christopher D. Manning. 2016. Compression of neural machine translation models via pruning. In *Proc. of The 20th SIGNLL Conference on Computational Natural Language Learning*, pages 291–301, Berlin, Germany. Association for Computational Linguistics. DOI: 10.18653/v1/k16-1029. 35, 36

Prithviraj Sen, Marina Danilevsky, Yunyao Li, Siddhartha Brahma, Matthias Boehm, Laura Chiticariu, and Rajasekar Krishnamurthy. 2020. Learning explainable linguistic expressions with neural inductive logic programming for sentence classification. In *Proc. of the 2020 Conference on Empirical Methods in Natural Language Processing (EMNLP)*, pages 4211–4221, Online. Association for Computational Linguistics. DOI: 10.18653/v1/2020.emnlp-main.345. 56, 59

Sofia Serrano and Noah A. Smith. 2019. Is attention interpretable? In *Proc. of the 57th Annual Meeting of the Association for Computational Linguistics*, pages 2931–2951, Florence, Italy. Association for Computational Linguistics. DOI: 10.18653/v1/p19-1282. 32

Sharath M. Shankaranarayana and Davor Runje. 2019. Alime: Autoencoder based approach for local interpretability. ArXiv 1909.02437. DOI: 10.1007/978-3-030-33607-3_49. 45, 51

Chihiro Shibata, Kei Uchiumi, and Daichi Mochihashi. 2020. How LSTM encodes syntax: Exploring context vectors and semi-quantization on natural text. In *Proc. of the 28th International Conference on Computational Linguistics*, pages 4033–4043, Barcelona, Spain (Online).

International Committee on Computational Linguistics. DOI: 10.18653/v1/2020.coling-main.356. 26

Kumar Shridhar, Harshil Jain, Akshat Agarwal, and Denis Kleyko. 2020. End to end binarized neural networks for text classification. In *Proc. of SustaiNLP: Workshop on Simple and Efficient Natural Language Processing*, pages 29–34, Online. Association for Computational Linguistics. DOI: 10.18653/v1/2020.sustainlp-1.4. 29

Avanti Shrikumar, Peyton Greenside, and Anshul Kundaje. 2017. Learning important features through propagating activation differences. In *Proc. of the 34th International Conference on Machine Learning*, volume 70 of *Proc. of Machine Learning Research*, pages 3145–3153, International Convention Centre, Sydney, Australia. PMLR. 5, 12, 17, 65

Karen Simonyan, Andrea Vedaldi, and Andrew Zisserman. 2014. Deep inside convolutional networks: Visualising image classification models and saliency maps. ArXiv 1312.6034. 5, 6, 12, 21

Anders Søgaard. 2016. Evaluating word embeddings with fMRI and eye-tracking. In *Proc. of the 1st Workshop on Evaluating Vector-Space Representations for NLP*, pages 116–121. DOI: 10.18653/v1/w16-2521. 43

Anders Søgaard, Sebastian Ebert, Jasmijn Bastings, and Katja Filippova. 2021. We need to talk about random splits. ArXiv 2005.00636. 64

Anders Søgaard and Yoav Goldberg. 2016. Deep multi-task learning with low level tasks supervised at lower layers. In *Proc. of the 54th Annual Meeting of the Association for Computational Linguistics (Volume 2: Short Papers)*, pages 231–235, Berlin, Germany. Association for Computational Linguistics. DOI: 10.18653/v1/p16-2038. 19

Anders Søgaard, Anders Johannsen, Barbara Plank, Dirk Hovy, and Hector Martínez Alonso. 2014. What's in a p-value in NLP? In *Proc. of the Eighteenth Conference on Computational Natural Language Learning*, pages 1–10, Ann Arbor, Michigan. Association for Computational Linguistics. DOI: 10.3115/v1/w14-1601. 54

Anders Søgaard, Hector Martinez, Jakob Elming, and Anders Johannsen. 2013. Using crowdsourcing to get representations based on regular expressions. In *Proc. of the 2013 Conference on Empirical Methods in Natural Language Processing*, pages 1476–1480, Seattle, Washington, Association for Computational Linguistics. 60, 73

Anders Søgaard, Ivan Vulić, Sebastian Ruder, and Manaal Faruqui. 2019. *Cross-Lingual Word Embeddings*, 2 edition. Synthesis Lectures on Human Language Technologies. Morgan & Claypool, United States. DOI: 10.2200/s00920ed2v01y201904hlt042. 43

Jost Tobias Springenberg, Alexey Dosovitskiy, Thomas Brox, and Martin Riedmiller. 2015. Striving for simplicity: The all convolutional net. ArXiv 1412.6806. 21

Hendrik Strobelt, Sebastian Gehrmann, Hanspeter Pfister, and Alexander M. Rush. 2017. Lstmvis: A tool for visual analysis of hidden state dynamics in recurrent neural networks. ArXiv 1606.07461. DOI: 10.1109/tvcg.2017.2744158. 5, 8, 31, 40, 72

Kai Sun, Dian Yu, Jianshu Chen, Dong Yu, Yejin Choi, and Claire Cardie. 2019. DREAM: A challenge data set and models for dialogue-based reading comprehension. *Transactions of the Association for Computational Linguistics*, 7:217–231. DOI: 10.1162/tacl_a_00264. 5, 12, 19

Mukund Sundararajan, Ankur Taly, and Qiqi Yan. 2017. Axiomatic attribution for deep networks. ArXiv 1703.01365. 5, 7, 12, 17, 23, 65

Madhumita Sushil, Simon Šuster, and Walter Daelemans. 2018. Rule induction for global explanation of trained models. In *Proc. of the 2018 EMNLP Workshop BlackboxNLP: Analyzing and Interpreting Neural Networks for NLP*, pages 82–97, Brussels, Belgium. Association for Computational Linguistics. DOI: 10.18653/v1/w18-5411. 3, 67

Ilya Sutskever, Oriol Vinyals, and Quoc V. Le. 2014. Sequence to sequence learning with neural networks. ArXiv 1409.3215. 16

Mirac Suzgun, Yonatan Belinkov, Stuart Shieber, and Sebastian Gehrmann. 2019. LSTM networks can perform dynamic counting. In *Proc. of the Workshop on Deep Learning and Formal Languages: Building Bridges*, pages 44–54, Florence. Association for Computational Linguistics. DOI: 10.18653/v1/w19-3905. 31

Raphael Tang, Yao Lu, and Jimmy Lin. 2019. Natural language generation for effective knowledge distillation. In *Proc. of the 2nd Workshop on Deep Learning Approaches for Low-Resource NLP (DeepLo 2019)*, pages 202–208, Hong Kong, China. Association for Computational Linguistics. DOI: 10.18653/v1/d19-6122. 53

Ian Tenney, Dipanjan Das, and Ellie Pavlick. 2019. Bert rediscovers the classical nlp pipeline. ArXiv 1905.05950. DOI: 10.18653/v1/p19-1452. 44, 66

Ian Tenney, James Wexler, Jasmijn Bastings, Tolga Bolukbasi, Andy Coenen, Sebastian Gehrmann, Ellen Jiang, Mahima Pushkarna, Carey Radebaugh, Emily Reif, and Ann Yuan. 2020. The language interpretability tool: Extensible, interactive visualizations and analysis for NLP models. In *Proc. of the 2020 Conference on Empirical Methods in Natural Language Processing: System Demonstrations*, pages 107–118, Online. Association for Computational Linguistics. DOI: 10.18653/v1/2020.emnlp-demos.15. 72

Marcos V. Treviso and André F. T. Martins. 2020. The explanation game: Towards prediction explainability through sparse communication. ArXiv 2004.13876. DOI: 10.18653/v1/2020.blackboxnlp-1.10. 36

Valentin Trifonov, Octavian-Eugen Ganea, Anna Potapenko, and Thomas Hofmann. 2018. Learning and evaluating sparse interpretable sentence embeddings. In *Proc. of the 2018 EMNLP Workshop BlackboxNLP: Analyzing and Interpreting Neural Networks for NLP*, pages 200–210, Brussels, Belgium. Association for Computational Linguistics. DOI: 10.18653/v1/w18-5422. 29

Thomas Alexander Trost and Dietrich Klakow. 2017. Parameter free hierarchical graph-based clustering for analyzing continuous word embeddings. In *Proc. of TextGraphs-11: the Workshop on Graph-based Methods for Natural Language Processing*, pages 30–38, Vancouver, Canada. Association for Computational Linguistics. DOI: 10.18653/v1/w17-2404. 5, 44

Joseph Turian, Lev-Arie Ratinov, and Yoshua Bengio. 2010. Word representations: A simple and general method for semi-supervised learning. In *Proc. of the 48th Annual Meeting of the Association for Computational Linguistics*, pages 384–394, Uppsala, Sweden. Association for Computational Linguistics. 16, 39

Shyam Upadhyay and Ming-Wei Chang. 2017. Annotating derivations: A new evaluation strategy and dataset for algebra word problems. In *Proc. of the 15th Conference of the European Chapter of the Association for Computational Linguistics: Volume 1, Long Papers*, pages 494–504, Valencia, Spain. Association for Computational Linguistics. DOI: 10.18653/v1/e17-1047. 61

Shikhar Vashishth, Shyam Upadhyay, Gaurav Singh Tomar, and Manaal Faruqui. 2019. Attention interpretability across nlp tasks. ArXiv 1909.11218. 12, 18, 32

Ashish Vaswani, Noam Shazeer, Niki Parmar, Jakob Uszkoreit, Llion Jones, Aidan N. Gomez, Łukasz Kaiser, and Illia Polosukhin. 2017. Attention is all you need. In *Advances in Neural Information Processing Systems*, 30:5998–6008. Curran Associates, Inc. 15, 31

Jesse Vig. 2019. A multiscale visualization of attention in the transformer model. In *Proc. of the 57th Annual Meeting of the Association for Computational Linguistics: System Demonstrations*, pages 37–42, Florence, Italy. Association for Computational Linguistics. DOI: 10.18653/v1/p19-3007. 71

Georgios Vlassopoulos. 2019. Decision boundary approximation: A new method for locally explaining predictions of complex classification models. Technical report, University of Leiden. 51

Elena Voita, David Talbot, Fedor Moiseev, Rico Sennrich, and Ivan Titov. 2019. Analyzing multi-head self-attention: Specialized heads do the heavy lifting, the rest can be pruned. In *Proc. of the 57th Annual Meeting of the Association for Computational Linguistics*, pages 5797–5808, Florence, Italy. Association for Computational Linguistics. DOI: 10.18653/v1/p19-1580. 2, 10, 12, 15, 18, 23, 36

Ivan Vulić, Sebastian Ruder, and Anders Søgaard. 2020. Are all good word vector spaces iso-morphic? In *Proc. of the 2020 Conference on Empirical Methods in Natural Language Processing (EMNLP)*, pages 3178–3192, Online. Association for Computational Linguistics. DOI: 10.18653/v1/2020.emnlp-main.257. 43

Sandra Wachter, Brent Mittelstadt, and Luciano Floridi. 2017. Why a Right to Explanation of Automated Decision-Making Does Not Exist in the General Data Protection Regulation. *International Data Privacy Law*, 7(2):76–99. DOI: 10.1093/idpl/ipx005. 68

David Wadden, Shanchuan Lin, Kyle Lo, Lucy Lu Wang, Madeleine van Zuylen, Arman Co-han, and Hannaneh Hajishirzi. 2020. Fact or fiction: Verifying scientific claims. ArXiv 2004.14974. DOI: 10.18653/v1/2020.emnlp-main.609. 73

Eric Wallace, Jens Tuyls, Junlin Wang, Sanjay Subramanian, Matt Gardner, and Sameer Singh. 2019. Allennlp interpret: A framework for explaining predictions of nlp models. ArXiv 1909.09251. DOI: 10.18653/v1/d19-3002. 71

J. Wang, W. Wang, and W. Gao. 2018. Beyond knowledge distillation: Collaborative learn-ing for bidirectional model assistance. *IEEE Access*, 6:39490–39500. DOI: 10.1109/access.2018.2854918. 53

Shuohang Wang and Jing Jiang. 2016. Learning natural language inference with LSTM. In *Proc. of the 2016 Conference of the North American Chapter of the Association for Computational Linguistics: Human Language Technologies*, pages 1442–1451, San Diego, California. Associa-tion for Computational Linguistics. DOI: 10.18653/v1/n16-1170. 31, 32

Alex Warstadt, Yu Cao, Ioana Grosu, Wei Peng, Hagen Blix, Yining Nie, Anna Alsop, Shikha Bordia, Haokun Liu, Alicia Parrish, Sheng-Fu Wang, Jason Phang, Anhad Mohananey, Phu Mon Htut, Paloma Jeretič, and Samuel R. Bowman. 2019. Investigating bert's knowledge of language: Five analysis methods with npis. ArXiv 1909.02597. DOI: 10.18653/v1/d19-1286. 49

Gail Weiss, Yoav Goldberg, and Eran Yahav. 2018. On the practical computational power of finite precision RNNs for language recognition. In *Proc. of the 56th Annual Meeting of the Association for Computational Linguistics (Volume 2: Short Papers)*, pages 740–745, Melbourne, Australia. Association for Computational Linguistics. DOI: 10.18653/v1/p18-2117. 15, 31

Sarah Wiegreffe and Ana Marasović. 2021. Teach me to explain: A review of datasets for explainable nlp. ArXiv 2102.12060. 73

Mike Wojnowicz, Ben Cruz, Xuan Zhao, Brian Wallace, Matt Wolff, Jay Luan, and Caleb Crable. 2016. influence sketching: Finding influential samples in large-scale regressions. *2016 IEEE International Conference on Big Data (Big Data)*. DOI: 10.1109/bigdata.2016.7841024. 46, 51

David H. Wolpert. 1996. The lack of A priori distinctions between learning algorithms. *Neural Computation*, 8(7):1341–1390. DOI: 10.1162/neco.1996.8.7.1341. 64

Yimeng Wu, Peyman Passban, Mehdi Rezagholizadeh, and Qun Liu. 2020. Why skip if you can combine: A simple knowledge distillation technique for intermediate layers. In *Proc. of the 2020 Conference on Empirical Methods in Natural Language Processing (EMNLP)*, pages 1016–1021, Online. Association for Computational Linguistics. DOI: 10.18653/v1/2020.emnlp-main.74. 32, 53

Xia Xiao, Zigeng Wang, and Sanguthevar Rajasekaran. 2019. Autoprune: Automatic network pruning by regularizing auxiliary parameters. In *Advances in Neural Information Processing Systems*, volume 32. Curran Associates, Inc. 28

Zhengnan Xie, Sebastian Thiem, Jaycie Martin, Elizabeth Wainwright, Steven Marmorstein, and Peter Jansen. 2020. WorldTree v2: A corpus of science-domain structured explanations and inference patterns supporting multi-hop inference. In *Proc. of the 12th Language Resources and Evaluation Conference*, pages 5456–5473, Marseille, France. European Language Resources Association. 73

Ziqing Yang, Yiming Cui, Zhipeng Chen, Wanxiang Che, Ting Liu, Shijin Wang, and Guoping Hu. 2020. TextBrewer: An Open-Source Knowledge Distillation Toolkit for Natural Language Processing. In *Proc. of the 58th Annual Meeting of the Association for Computational Linguistics: System Demonstrations*, pages 9–16, Online. Association for Computational Linguistics. DOI: 10.18653/v1/2020.acl-demos.2. 72

Chih-Kuan Yeh, Cheng-Yu Hsieh, Arun Sai Suggala, David I. Inouye, and Pradeep Ravikumar. 2019. On the (in)fidelity and sensitivity for explanations. ArXiv 1901.09392. 59

Chih-Kuan Yeh, Joon Sik Kim, Ian E. H. Yen, and Pradeep Ravikumar. 2018. Representer point selection for explaining deep neural networks. ArXiv 1811.09720. 5, 44, 46, 47

David Yenicelik, Florian Schmidt, and Yannic Kilcher. 2020. How does BERT capture semantics? a closer look at polysemous words. In *Proc. of the Third BlackboxNLP Workshop on Analyzing and Interpreting Neural Networks for NLP*, pages 156–162, Online. Association for Computational Linguistics. DOI: 10.18653/v1/2020.blackboxnlp-1.15. 5, 44

Seul-Ki Yeom, Philipp Seegerer, Sebastian Lapuschkin, Alexander Binder, Simon Wiedemann, Klaus-Robert Müller, and Wojciech Samek. 2020. Pruning by explaining: A novel criterion for deep neural network pruning. ArXiv 1912.08881. DOI: 10.1016/j.patcog.2021.107899. 25

Haonan Yu, Sergey Edunov, Yuandong Tian, and Ari S. Morcos. 2020. Playing the lottery with rewards and multiple languages: lottery tickets in RL and NLP. In *International Conference on Learning Representations*. 27

Rowan Zellers, Yonatan Bisk, Ali Farhadi, and Yejin Choi. 2019. From recognition to cognition: Visual commonsense reasoning. ArXiv 1811.10830. DOI: 10.1109/cvpr.2019.00688. 74

John Zerilli, Alistair Knott, James Maclaurin, and Colin Gavaghan. 2018. Transparency in algorithmic and human decision-making: Is there a double standard? *Philosophy & Technology*, 32(4):661–683. DOI: 10.1007/s13347-018-0330-6. 68

Matthew Shunshi Zhang and Bradly Stadie. 2019. One-shot pruning of recurrent neural networks by jacobian spectrum evaluation. ArXiv 1912.00120. 35

Xinyang Zhang, Ningfei Wang, Hua Shen, Shouling Ji, Xiapu Luo, and Ting Wang. 2019. Interpretable deep learning under fire. 58

Yu Zhang, Peter Tiňo, Aleš Leonardis, and Ke Tang. 2020. A survey on neural network interpretability. ArXiv 2012.14261. 4, 5, 8, 11

Mengjie Zhao, Tao Lin, Fei Mi, Martin Jaggi, and Hinrich Schütze. 2020. Masking as an efficient alternative to finetuning for pretrained language models. In *Proc. of the 2020 Conference on Empirical Methods in Natural Language Processing (EMNLP)*, pages 2226–2241, Online. Association for Computational Linguistics. DOI: 10.18653/v1/2020.emnlp-main.174. 28

Xiang Zhou, Yixin Nie, Hao Tan, and Mohit Bansal. 2020. The curse of performance instability in analysis datasets: Consequences, source, and suggestions. In *Proc. of the 2020 Conference on Empirical Methods in Natural Language Processing (EMNLP)*, pages 8215–8228, Online. Association for Computational Linguistics. DOI: 10.18653/v1/2020.emnlp-main.659. 54

Michael Zhu and Suyog Gupta. 2017. To prune, or not to prune: exploring the efficacy of pruning for model compression. ArXiv 1710.01878. 26

Xunjie Zhu and Gerard de Melo. 2020. Sentence analogies: Linguistic regularities in sentence embeddings. In *Proc. of the 28th International Conference on Computational Linguistics*, pages 3389–3400, Barcelona, Spain (Online). International Committee on Computational Linguistics. DOI: 10.18653/v1/2020.coling-main.300. 40

Author's Biography

ANDERS SØGAARD

Anders Søgaard is a father of three and a published poet, as well as a Full Professor in Computer Science the University of Copenhagen. He is currently funded by the Novo Nordisk Foundation, the Lundbeck Foundation, and the Innovation Fund Denmark; before that, he held an ERC Starting Grant and a Google Focused Research Award. He has won best paper awards at NAACL, EACL, CoNLL, etc. He previously wrote *Semi-Supervised Learning and Domain Adaptation in NLP* (Morgan & Claypool, 2013) and *Cross-Lingual Word Embeddings* (Morgan & Claypool, 2019), the latter with co-authors Ivan Vulić, Sebastian Ruder, and Manaal Faruqui.

Printed in the United States
by Baker & Taylor Publisher Services